In Loving Memory of

Dennis L. Shippey

Husband to Linda

Father to Scott and Sondra

Grandfather to Ian, Luke, Mia, Aaron and Hannah

Scott, Linda, Dennis and Sondra
Bruce Rollins far right
2011

Contents   Page

Forward	4
Before the Knock	6
The Knock	9
Early Onset vs Early Stage Alzheimer's	10
The Missed Engagement	12
Scheduled Testing	16
Telling the Right People	20
Physical Activity: Engagement with Others	24
Activities for Daily Living	29
Support Groups	36
Recognizing Emotional Limits	40
"Angels" of Support and Respite	43
Changes in the Job	45
Sundowning	49
Driving Concerns	52
Cycling Challenges	59
The Hurricane	64
The Long Hospital Stay	69
Missing Person: The Lucky Bark	75
Adult Protective Services	84
Visiting with Law Enforcement	86
Alzheimer's Organization & D.C. Conference	89
Jail, Bonds and Courts	93
Institute for Living	102
Veteran's Benefits PTSD	107
Transition to Dementia Care Facility	111
Pine Tree Cottage	114
Hospice Care	120
Journey's End	125
Brain Donation	129
Legacy of a Coach	134
About the Author	139
Appendix	141

Forward

Since Dennis' passing in 2011, this story has continuously floated in my mind. I knew I had to share the experience of what I learned the hard way. But where do I begin with a story like this? I journaled a bit and then had a family friend help me set up a blog. My entries on the blog have helped me stay in touch with the experiences that were mine from 2002, when we got the diagnosis of Early Onset Alzheimer's.

My story will address the specific challenges when the one diagnosed is young, athletic, healthy and extremely active. I address the challenges of maintaining quality of life, driving concerns, hospital administration, law enforcement response, and various support groups. Most of what I learned was under great duress, yet it doesn't need to be that way.

It's a story I wish I knew nothing about. "Still Alice" and "The Notebook" are just movies for many. They are sad stories that enlighten folks for a couple of hours about this devastating diagnosis that 'knocked on my door'. All things you experience in life are for a reason. They will make you or break you, and at times the breaking was heavy on my soul. But when there is no choice but to be strong and to be an advocate for dementia, that is what you do. Not my strength, but my strength through God carried me through those years.

This story is intended to act only as a resource for the caregiver. Every case is different. The stories will vary. But as an educator, I can't help but believe that good can come from sharing what I learned during my years as caregiver. If only one person benefits from anything I have presented, it has been well worth the time I spent reliving and writing about what I learned. And equally important, is that the caregiver needs to know there is someone who understands the emotional, physical and financial challenges that are inevitable.

Linda Shippey

Before the Knock

It was the fall of 1962 when I first met Dennis. We were sophomores in an English Literature class. I soon became attracted to this shy and polite young man. We dated throughout our high school years and stumbled through his college years at Eastern New Mexico University. After graduating from college in 1969, he took a coaching position at the new Dubuque Hempstead High School. On February 7, 1970 we were married, and he left later that month for his active military service that was a result of being drafted into the U.S. Army. Fast forward past Vietnam, and we were a young couple with one child and another one on the way while he attended graduate school at the University of Northern Iowa.

After graduate school, we spent a short time in Elkhart, Indiana, and Davenport, Iowa, before moving our young family to Pasadena, Texas, where Dennis would be a coach for both boys' and girls' swimming. Before he flew to Pasadena, Dennis said "I want you to go with me, because if you won't be happy there, we won't go". My response was simply that I would not know if I would like it or not just in one visit, but if he wanted the job, we would move our family because it was important to me that he follow his dreams.

Our move to Texas took us 1100 miles away from our parents and extended family. Since Dennis had been in New Mexico for college, the move away did not concern him as his excitement for the new job was an answer to prayer. (Returning from Vietnam he could not find a coaching/teaching job so he did odd jobs.)

As it turned out, the move to Texas was a blessing in disguise. Even though I was homesick for family, I kept myself busy and soon was attending a nearby junior college in the evenings while Dennis watched the children. At his encouragement, I finished my teaching degree at the University of Houston/Clear Lake, and eventually went back to complete a Master's degree in Supervision and Mid-Management (Principal certification).

The community embraced our family with numerous opportunities to manage community swimming pools and coach summer swim programs. The high school coaching position was exactly what Dennis had hoped for and more.

His commitment to the Pasadena ISD swim program took an additional turn when he accepted the position as Aquatic Coordinator for the four high schools. He took the position with the understanding that he could remain coach for J. Frank Dobie High School.

While Dennis was coaching, my teaching degree provided numerous opportunities as well. For ten years I taught 6th grade math, then I moved to be one of four teachers selected to start up an alternative school for grades 6-8. Two years later I returned to an 8th grade math position. When the district was looking for a technology trainer for teachers, I applied as a teacher advocate, addressing the needs for effective implementation of technology instruction in the classroom. At the encouragement of my district level administrators and Dennis, I started interviewing for assistant principal positions and soon accepted assignments at both elementary and intermediate schools.

Our life in Texas became filled with family life and careers. Raising and educating our two children was a high priority ...both are Texas A&M graduates. Dennis loved to cycle, and for more than 20 years he rode his bicycle to school for exercise. In the summer we managed swimming pools, coached swimming with an age-group program, taught swim lessons and spent every free minute out in our boat water skiing with family and friends.

With our busy careers, it became evident that we needed some quality time together. Budget-minded Dennis started the date night, with him cutting practice short on Friday's, so we could get to the movie before 6:00 pm. That became non-negotiable unless someone was sick or we had an unexpected commitment. Later we made friends with a couple who took country western dance classes. Dennis was excited to do anything country because he loved the music. Lesson after lesson we became more and more hooked on this new activity. Eventually we were dancing three to four nights a week. It was great fun, quality time and exercise. Whether boating, dancing, movies or biking (I did join him at times) ... we had fun! We enjoyed each others' company and were best friends. Even with the occasional hiccups in a relationship, our marriage was rock solid. There was nothing we couldn't talk about and face together with faith.

Our married life was everything I dreamed for and more. I had an occasional thought that our life was almost too perfect, something terrible was going to happen.

The Knock

When a stranger comes knocking, you take a peek before opening the door. You are cautious because the unknown is standing before you. Who is this stranger? Does he have the wrong address? How can I help him be on his way? But with no signs of imminent danger... you address the stranger with a cordial greeting.

Once the conversation starts, it is evident that this stranger has a message for you. The message will impact your life and the lives of others forever.

Reluctantly, the two of you sit down to a conversation that will shatter life as you have known it. The facts will mean certain changes in life for your entire family. The details of how to make adjustments and live life fully will be lacking, but they must be out there somewhere.

After sharing the news, the stranger admits how difficult it has been to share this news but knew it had to be done. You question, "Could there be a mistake?" "Do you have the wrong house?" (And the most important question is, "What do we do now?"). The answers become apparent. No mistake. Not the wrong address. The details for what we do now would begin to unfold as you stumble and fall but remain steadfast with the one you love.

Alzheimer's/dementia is a life sentence for everyone involved. A life unknown and unfamiliar to the person who opened the door.

Early-Onset vs Early-Stage Alzheimers

This story is written from my perspective as caregiver and wife. It was May 2002 when the doctor shared the findings of all tests that led to the diagnosis of Early Onset Alzheimer's.

Early Stage refers to people, irrespective of age, who are diagnosed with Alzheimer's disease or related disorders and are in the beginning stages of the disease. In this stage they retain the ability to participate in daily activities and a give-and-take dialogue. This includes those persons with "younger-onset" that develop dementia under age of 65 and are in the early stages of the disease.

Younger-onset Alzheimer's, also known as early-onset Alzheimer's, refers to those individuals younger than age 65 who have a diagnosis. People with Early Onset often face challenges that include career, children at home, and finances.

There is no certainty for the diagnosis until death and only an autopsy can confirm the findings. Dementia itself can be caused by a multitude of things: Vascular disease, Lewy Bodies, Pick's disease, Parkinson's disease and others. My experiences from 2002 to 2011 were complicated by the age and fitness of a man in his prime. He had good habits for health, exercise and nutrition that would be above that of most people his age. As a high school swim coach and Aquatic Director, he had a successful and productive career. He was extremely active and had been to the doctor for nothing more than the flu or a physical.

10

For the first five years, denial was the false protector of what was to come. Small adjustments to daily routines helped keep things somewhat "normal". There were calendars, reminders (written and verbal), and support from family/friends.

But during the last four years, there were major changes that would blindside me and my husband. I will share these things I learned, things I did wrong, things that were frightening, things that were violent, and things that would involve law enforcement, hospital staffers, doctors and community. I will share tips of how the caregiver might simplify the daily routines, and how to be prepared for the challenges that come with dementia.

The Missed Engagement

It was somewhere in February or March 2002 when I started noticing little things that Dennis would forget. There was a period of time when Dennis would misplace and/or forget things. He was constantly saying, "Where is my..."; "What happened to my...." and "Where are you....". As a wife, I found these things a little annoying and out of the norm for him, so I just did what I could to help resolve the issues.

We had just built a new home and moved into our dream retirement home. Dennis was coaching and dealing with helping our daughter Sondra settle into our old house that she bought. He knew there were some issues with the house, so one by one he took care of those issues. The biggest project at her home was the piping in the attic. Parts needed repair, so he decided to replace the old pipes with new PVC.

The PVC cement generated strong fumes that were concerning to Sondra. She insisted her dad wear a mask because the fumes coming down from the attic were strong. It was January/February so the heat wasn't a problem, but poor ventilation in the attic was a concern for all of us. So Dennis took his time, working a few hours each day, and after about two weeks he completed the job.

You may ask yourself, how is this relevant to the story? It was only a few weeks later that I noticed an increase in what I assumed were hearing issues.

During that time, I was an Assistant Principal at an intermediate school. Dennis usually stopped by to eat lunch while I was on cafeteria duty. With our busy schedules, it was nice to grab a bite and remind one another of the evening schedule. On one particular day, I reminded him we had a dinner engagement at the University of Houston for a friend who was graduating from Culinary School. There was a formal dinner, and we were looking forward to the festivities with friends. I reminded him twice to meet me at our daughter's house by 5:30 p.m., so we could make it to the dinner on time. No questions were asked, and he assured me that he would see me then.

At 5:30 p.m., I sat at my daughter's house waiting. I waited and I waited. I was frustrated because I made numerous calls and could not reach him by phone. (He had lost his cell phone.) Finally, we had no choice but to drive on to the University of Houston at 6:00 p.m. I continued calling as my friend drove. Finally there was a pleasant calm voice answering the phone at our home. It was Dennis! He said, "Where are you?" That question just set me off, so I blasted, "What do you mean where am I? I am on my way to the dinner, and because of you we are going to be late!" He rebounded with, "I have no idea what you are talking about." To that I sighed and said, "Well just stay there, and I will see you at home after the dinner!" I couldn't believe it! All the reminders and he had forgotten.

That evening we discussed the confusion, and he apologized in the midst of me fussing at him. I told him that I thought maybe he should go to the doctor for a hearing test. Honestly, I was not being sarcastic! He was a Vietnam Veteran, and I always believed he had some legitimate hearing issues from the big howitzer guns. A year of working fire missions with the 101st Airborne were bound to have damaged his hearing. He reluctantly agreed; that next day I set up the appointment we could both attend.

On the day of the appointment, Dennis and I walked into our doctor 's office to discuss possible hearing concerns. Hearing was checked promptly, and it was fine. Back in the exam room, the doctor asked me why I thought there was a problem. Dennis said, "Oh she is just upset because I forgot a dinner date". Feeling like a total fool, I blurted out the things I had noticed recently. When I added that Dennis was such a considerate person and I knew he was not purposely choosing to ignore things, the doctor decided to just check a few other things.

A nurse came in and asked a battery of questions. She asked him to count backwards from 100 by fives; what year was it; who was president; when was his birthday. He had to repeat back a series of words to her and so on. The more she did this, the more irritated Dennis became. He was having difficulty and covered it by saying, "This is all stupid and a waste of time". She then gave him a sheet of paper and pencil. Her directions were to write down anything he wanted to. I thought to myself that she has no idea what he could write. I knew he was frustrated. I knew he was angry at me for making the appointment. So I started to walk out when she said, "Do you want to see what he wrote?" I declined, then she assured me that I did. On that paper he had written,

"I LOVE MY WIFE!" With that my heart ached. I felt foolish. Since we had driven separately, I excused myself because I thought we were done, and I drove on home.

I cried softly while driving home thinking I had just put him through all that frustration and humiliation for nothing. Once home, I sat in the recliner resting and wondering what our conversation would be when he arrived. How could I make him understand how sorry I was. Dennis arrived about 25 minutes later. He came in and leaned over to give me a kiss. He said, "Well the doctor must think something is wrong because he has scheduled me for some other appointments. I am not mad at you. I love you."

[What I learned: When there was an abundance of confusion where previously there had been none, I had to find out why. Many times early warning signs are missed. Simple things like confusion over misplaced items is not out of the ordinary. But when you see or sense that things in the daily routine are no longer routine, listen to your "gut". An appointment and trip to the doctor can put your mind at ease. However, early detection of memory issues is important to the medical intervention.]

Scheduled Testing

Going forward, Dennis was faced with countless appointments for medical testing. At no time during all the testing did we have any idea where all this was leading. It was simply explained that memory issues can be caused by various medical conditions. A proper diagnosis would require patience on our part, and a willingness to follow through on all testing.

His first appointment was with the neurologist who did a thorough physical exam and once again repeated a battery of questions and mental exercises in the office. Tests performed included complete blood work, EEG, CT scans, MRI and PET scan. This took a few weeks to schedule and complete. Since Dennis was feeling well, we joked about how this was probably just a waste of time, but at least we would have a great baseline for good health.

The final appointment was with a neuropsychiatrist in Galveston. Never missing a good reason to take a drive to Galveston, we actually looked forward to seeing the beach and having a relaxing day. Neither of us knew what was involved in this testing nor how it would be administered. When we arrived, the doctor greeted us and sat down in a waiting area to explain how the test would be administered and that it would take three to five hours. That was a shock! I could see the look on Dennis' face. He was already at wits end with all the testing. He just wanted it over and behind him. The doctor went on to say that I could not accompany Dennis during the testing. They would take a lunch break returning early afternoon to complete the exam. He tried to lighten the mood by sharing with Dennis that astronauts had taken this test and some of the humorous things about that.

Dennis reluctantly left with the doctor. I sensed his agitation and frustration, so I had some concerns whether he would be cooperative when they started asking that series of questions we heard in our doctor's office, and the neurologist's office. I read a few magazines to put my mind at ease. When that didn't work, I gazed out the window at a beautiful day full of life and the bustling medical center. I couldn't help but wonder by then ... what was happening? What did they suspect? Here was a man who was in perfect health, who ate healthy, who exercised, who seemed to do all the right things. He was a godly man and brought so much love, support and encouragement to many as a husband, father, grandfather, coach, and friend. Obviously, I was starting to be concerned but never expected anything life threatening.

After about two hours, the doctor and Dennis returned. It was clear the testing was met with frustration and agitation. I could see on Dennis' face that he was ready to get out of there. The doctor explained that Dennis needed a break. He suggested a leisurely lunch and to return so they could complete the testing. As we left the medical center, Dennis was clearly irritated. He explained he was tired of people making him feel stupid with crazy questions and puzzles. He was never one who was fond of card games, puzzles, word games and such, so this format of testing made everything worse. While at lunch, we talked about the testing. He was insistent NOT to return and just go home. I appealed to his concern for family and suggested he was doing this for us. He came back at me with, "Then you go in there and let him ask you those questions and see how it makes you feel. I don't need this shit!" With much prompting, and a few sincere expressions of love and concern, he finally agreed and we returned.

The total time invested in testing and appointments took about six weeks. Next came the meeting with our family physician for a report and results on everything. We were told everything on all tests was good. It seemed like great news! But then there was a pause. He explained that what they had been doing was testing for and eliminating any other possible explanation for what was happening. The neuropsych test had clearly identified a diminished cognitive level to be associated with a person who has the IQ of about 85. Since we were both educators that was familiar, but alarming to us. The doctor went on to say that with Dennis having a masters degree, he would be expected to have a much higher cognitive ability. Therefore, every possible diagnosis that would explain this had been eliminated other than EARLY ONSET ALZHEIMER'S. With those few words (EOA), our life came to a screeching halt. For a few minutes, time stood still. The doctor continued giving us valuable information that we were trying to process.

A plan of treatment was laid out in detail. Dennis would start taking Exelon. The first month he would take 1.5 mg per day; the next month 3.0 mg per day; next would be 4.5 mg per day and finally he would reach the optimum dose of 6.0 mg per day. The doctor explained he believed the Alzheimer's was caught early. He asked if we had long term care insurance. I sighed and explained we had just dropped it due to financial constraints. We were numb with confusion so when asked if we had any questions ... there were none. We didn't know enough to ask a question. This diagnosis had NEVER crossed our minds.

As we walked out of the office, I remember Dennis taking my hand and saying, "If this is true, it is YOU I feel sorry for because you will have to take care of me." I just gave him a kiss on the cheek and said not to worry about that. As we got in the car, I was at a loss for words. The silence was deafening. I said, "Hey I have a great idea, let's go get a manicure/pedicure. Are you game?" He chuckled and readily agreed to get pampered that way for the first time ever.

This date was May 2002. Dennis was only 56 years old.

[What I learned: Ask questions about the tests that are being scheduled and how those results will be used. Ask questions about the role of the neurologist and the neuropsychiatrist and their procedures. If you understand what each appointment/test is targeting, you can be better informed and prepared to ask appropriate questions. The goal is to find a cause for the memory impairment.]

Telling the Right People

Along with the diagnosis came a great deal of responsibility. Not just for ourselves, but for our family and our education/professional community.

My first thoughts were to let our children know. Our grown children were going to be a huge part of our support network, so of course they were told first. In the beginning, there wasn't much to share except that a diagnosis and the medical treatment had been presented. Many questions came as the weeks passed, so we were all on the Internet searching for answers to a disease that was foreign to our minds. Such an announcement was met with silence first; then "Are they sure?"; and "What does this mean?"

At the same time, I was making sure our extended family knew of the diagnosis. Dennis' younger brother and I spoke candidly about keeping this news from his mother until later because she would worry. For my immediate siblings, it was imperative they knew what we were facing because their support would be critical for me to maintain a sense of normalcy for the months and years to come. When I look back on sharing this diagnosis with others, it would have been best had Dennis initiated those conversations. Ideally, I would be his support in that difficult conversation. But in our case, he was in total denial. He didn't believe it and refused to accept the diagnosis. No way would he tell anyone. Unfortunately, that left me to make the decisions who to tell, what to tell and when to tell.

As a school administrator, I knew I had to advise district administrators of this recent diagnosis. Since Dennis was the Aquatic Coordinator for the district, I first spoke with Superintendent to whom I was close, and of course, notified the principal of Dennis' high school. What was expected, of course, was a letter from the doctor stating that Dennis was still capable of carrying out his duties as specified in his contract. That was not a problem, and the doctor was glad to do so. With all that in place, it was the end of school year 2002, so our summer vacation began.

The regiment of Exelon started that summer and it was not without its setbacks. Dennis started to lose weight and he slept more than usual. We spent most of our summer visiting our families in Iowa. Because we were staying with Dennis' mother, she inquired as to why he was sleeping so much. Her concern was for some ailment that needed attention. As hard as it was, I told her the diagnosis and the treatment Dennis was following. At 80+ years old, she was shocked because no one she knew had ever had this diagnosis. She had more questions than I had answers at that point. As I reflect on that decision to tell her, I wish Dennis had been with us in that conversation. I don't believe the two of them ever spoke about this.

I assured her we were going to be okay, and I would be taking good care of Dennis. I would make sure he had the best medical treatment (even though at the time I had no idea what that really meant).

Outside family and career personnel, sharing information

with people was complicated. Dennis was still active in his career as a high school swim coach and Aquatic Coordinator. With a high profile position in the community/district, news traveled quickly, near and far. Sometimes it was just trivial gossip being passed on. For a few individuals, it was an opportunity to attack Dennis' on the job. And eventually, all of this took away from the quality of life that was still present. And of course some friends, family, and neighbors pulled away from the whole situation because it was the unknown and uncomfortable to deal with. At the same time, there were individuals who were not close friends, neighbors we did not know and total strangers who stepped up to help and support both Dennis and myself.

This is not a journey in life that can be managed in isolation or alone. Sharing with neighbors and friends and distant family becomes a critical part of support. We began to treasure the faith, hope and love that was part of our lives --- in a new way that we could never have imagined.

At times, the negative impact on the job was that Dennis was defending himself in minor issues that were of no real consequence. I remember one particular situation where someone I trusted had taken a lead in criticizing and finding fault with Dennis instead of helping out or contacting me. I called our son Scott crying about the feeling of betrayal. He said, "Mom don't be mad at that person. You gave her information she didn't know how to handle. We don't even know what to do with this information. Pull yourself together because there are going to be more serious issues ahead of us. It's going to be okay." 22

[What I learned: Think carefully and collaborate with immediate family as to the who, what, when and how to share the diagnosis with others. Whatever you share and with whom is a challenging decision for you as a caregiver/family. Initially, you are struggling to deal with the news and the reality of your future needs. So it is important to realize others may/will struggle with the information also. Some will use the information to support and encourage. Others may use it as painful gossip that will make it difficult to maintain any resemblance of quality living. Be careful. Have a plan you and the family can support. And, if possible, involve the affected person in the conversations telling others. Doing so will help that person come to terms with the diagnosis.]

Physical Activity and Engagement with Others

Just before our retirement in 2004, Dennis and I were attending a Texas Senior Games swim meet in Temple, Texas. He was a lifelong competitive swimmer and coach. In 2000, he started attending meets for seniors just to get together with friends and have a good time. The fact he was a seasoned competitor made it even that much more fun.

At that meet, none of the competitors knew of the diagnosis for Dennis. Just like I did for my kids when they were young swimmers, I made sure Dennis got entered in his events and registered. At the meet, I wrote his event numbers and lane assignments on his arm so he wouldn't forget.

All was well until I heard the gun go off, and I looked up to see that Dennis was busy talking and had missed his event. Then in a flash -- I revisited my occasional thoughts that once Dennis couldn't follow the organization of swim meets, he would be "lost" to our world. Tears just fell down my cheek as I rushed to the other end of the pool. I approached the ongoing conversation with a declaration that he had just missed his event. To his shock, he could see I was correct. We walked back to our seats to regroup. You see -- in this meet if you miss an event, you are out of the rest of the meet. Just then a tall, and I mean very tall man, approached us. He asked me what was wrong and I explained.

He hurried off to speak with the officials and Dennis was placed back in the meet. The man who approached us was Bruce Rollins. As a kid, Bruce lived in nearby Iowa City and competed against Dennis in summer and high school meets. He told me he always looked up to Dennis and wanted to beat him. When we had time, I told him the diagnosis and what we were facing. He said, "Don't you worry about anything. Denny is my buddy. I will take care of the issues here at meets. And I will do my best to make sure he swims as long as he can. You just relax and cheer for him. I will do the rest." And so that friendship took on a whole new function.

Here is where I say that God walked into our picture. Well, you know what I mean. He was always there but I was trying desperately to monitor and be in charge of everything myself. Without a doubt, I knew he was an answer to prayer. Dennis loved this guy. He had never been one to hang out with guy friends. He was more of a loner or with family. But with Bruce it was different. Bruce cared for him like a brother.

This relationship was powerful and a blessing for both of us. For the next four years, Bruce did all he could to keep Dennis swimming. It gave me time for respite, and they were having a blast. Bruce picked the meets, the events and made all traveling arrangements. They roomed together as they traveled together. Bruce assured me he could monitor the meds and any other needs Dennis might have while traveling. It was his goal and my goal that Dennis enjoy every bit of swimming that time would allow. There were times when they had their challenges. Bruce told me that one time at a meet, they were leaving the hotel for the pool and he asked Dennis if he had his swim suit. He didn't. They tore the room apart looking

25

in every possible nook and cranny. Then Bruce said to him, "Dennis do you have your swimsuit on?" He did a quick check and smiled, "Yes I do!"

Dennis and Bruce traveled to Texas Senior Games, YMCA Nationals, and Masters Nationals for an incredibly high performance in swimming. During those years of competition (and with the help of Bruce and his buddies), Dennis was a national champion in all three levels of competition. In fact, when Dennis was inducted into the Texas Senior Games Hall of Fame for swimming (just a few weeks before his passing), Bruce announced that Dennis was ranked in the top five in the World in the FINA ranking for the breaststroke. Neither Dennis nor I were aware of that ranking. For Dennis it was all about swimming, the people that he met, and the fun of competing.

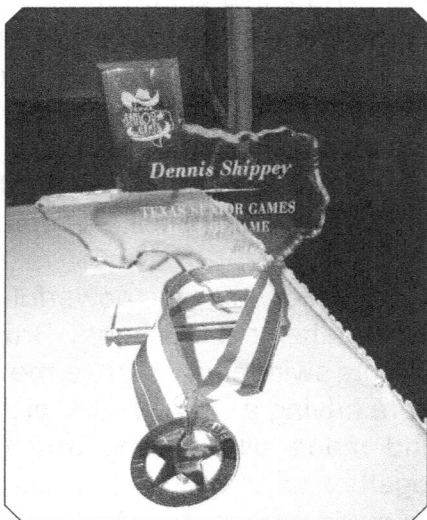

Swimming was God's gift to Dennis and the connection that made him an inspiration to others, as a coach, friend, neighbor and family man. Doctors were amazed that he was so strong and did so well. They attributed his athleticism, his engagement with others, his goal setting and his positive attitude for his ability to live a quality of life beyond expectations.

26

The following letter was written by Bruce Rollins to the TISCA coaches association shortly before Dennis' passing:

"To all of my friends who I have regaled with stories for years and/or know of Denny Shippey, my Iowa friend and swimming buddy for many years who was diagnosed with Alzheimer's disease at the age of 56, please say a prayer or two for him and his family. Denny metaphorically is on his last lap with 3-10 days to live. He has been in and out of hospitals for the past 2 years and it appears that his body cannot fight for much longer all of the things that have taken over his bodily functions. His lovely wife Linda called me this morning and let me know that the doctors who have fought so hard to make Denny comfortable and to continue functioning have recommended hospice care. In a sense, this is merciful for Denny who has had to endure a lot.

Those of you who knew him will remember him as a great and humble swimmer, willing to swim whatever we asked of him on relays, despite the fact that in 2007 and 2008 he was ranked as the 4th and 5th fastest 50 Meter Long Course breaststroker in the world by FINA in his age group. He honestly just loved swimming with all of us at meets and looked forward to them. Others will remember him as a great high school swim coach who was honored by the Texas Interscholastic Swim Coaches Association with their highest coaching award. As late as last summer, he was selected to the Texas Senior Games Hall of Fame, the first single sport swimmer ever selected. Finally, others will just remember him as Bruce's friend who was virtually inseparable from me at swim meets over the past 10 years. It has been one heck of an experience for all of us who knew him and supported him with kindness.

May God bless all of you and look after Denny and his family as he gets ready for his next event. I will let you know when he leaves the blocks."

Dennis Shippey and Bruce Rollins

[What I learned: Accept the help of others. It is difficult to believe that others can protect and care for your loved one as well as you do. But the doctors will tell you not to take on these challenges alone. Take care of yourself. If those you expected to support you disappear, that would be normal. It isn't that they do not care, they just may not be able to handle the unknown. On the other hand, there may/hopefully will be at least one person who steps up to give you respite care. And hopefully it will be a person who your loved one feels a closeness with. In my case, Dennis would never have allowed a stranger to "babysit" him, but a friend spending time with him was perfect.]

Activities for Daily Living

Noticeable changes to daily life became more evident after the first couple years. There were changes in organization, dressing, eating, hygiene and sleeping. We just made adjustments according to what was becoming difficult with time.

For work, it became apparent that I would help Dennis with his schedule and keep his papers organized. This seemed to help him continue working. Without a doubt, I believe other high school coaches were stepping up to help Dennis when they noticed any difficulties he had with completing tasks in a timely manner. The support was there with the administration, the coaches and myself.

On a more personal basis, the cell phone was the first casualty. Misplacing first then later losing a few cell phones made it obvious that the phone was difficult to manage. Regardless of how important it was for me to have constant ability to call Dennis, it was not possible for him to keep it with him, on him, or near him. After losing a few phones, we gave up. It was made easier when I was able to put tracking phones hard-wired in our vehicles so I could have constant computer access to his location.

At home, organization of his personal items was another observed change. Dennis had always been meticulous with every detail regarding his clothing and personal items. He had his own walk-in closet so I didn't pay much attention to those areas. What I did start to notice was that he was 'hoarding' or 'gathering' unusual items in his drawers. I would find napkins, kleenex, papers, unopened mail, books, magazines,trinkets, and, at times even crazy little items of mine in his drawers or in his closet.

After retirement and about four years into this disease, I noticed some peculiar dressing changes. Dennis would put on socks that didn't match, shoes that didn't match, warm clothes when it was hot, and shorts when it was cold. It was not a huge issue but one that I would bring to his attention. I hated seeing him with those mismatched socks so I just got rid of all his socks and bought all new ones exactly the same. I limited his items of clothing depending on the weather. I put away shoes that could be mismatched. In other words, I gave him less choices. All of these decisions kept his independence in tact and my concerns over these little details were put to rest.

During the night time hours, he started experiencing sundowning. Medically, sundowning is described as a psychological phenomenon that occurs as the sun goes down and is associated with increased confusion and restlessness (because things look less familiar in the dusk/dark).

When Dennis began wandering aimlessly during the night, we discussed the option of putting locks high on the doors so he could not get outside at night. I didn't go through with that safety issue since I had an alarm on all doors and windows. There were a couple of times when he went outside during the night (sometimes to the backyard, other times to the front), but with the alarm I could intervene and guide him back to the bedroom or bathroom.

About seven years into the challenge of Alzheimer's, the nighttime wandering became more aggressive. I could only guess that he would wake from dreams that took him back to Vietnam and combat. He would jump up in the bed and scream for me to watch out for the snakes. I would find him wandering around on the floor looking under the bed for 'something'. Other times he would wake up shouting in anger. I did my best at calming him.

One of the worst nighttime experiences was when he woke up after midnight -- ran to the bedroom door hitting it and slamming on walls. He was screaming in complete rage that made no sense. I had NEVER seen him like this. "I am sick and tired of people making me feel stupid. There is nothing wrong with me!! Quit treating me this way. This has to stop!." I followed him to the kitchen trying to reassure him and calm him, yet he continued the tirade. I distanced myself from him, with the kitchen island separating us. It seemed as though time stood still in rage. That was the first time he exhibited extremely verbal and violent outbursts and attacks on property. I kept asking Dennis, "Are you going to hurt me? Please stop .. you are scaring me." He screamed no, he wasn't going to hurt me, as he approached me cowering in the corner of the kitchen. As the tirade continued, I slowly worked my way to the phone. Without much thought I called Scott for safety. He could hear the ranting and the rage that made him suggest I call the police. I responded with concerns of fear for what they might do if they came. Scott said, "At least get out of the house." I replied that I would try. I got around to my keys and headed to the garage for the car. Dennis followed me and as I got in the car and locked the doors, the rage increased because I was backing out of the garage. Dennis beat on the car with reckless abandon in a seizure state that had no meaningful trigger. I drove out the gate of our community and called our daughter Sondra to come help. I explained what had happened and assured her I would wait before returning to the house.

When Sondra and her husband arrived, we drove back to the house. Dennis had calmed and was pacing quietly in the kitchen. The four of us sat at the dining room table and let Dennis speak. We assured him we loved him and that his unexpected anger was alarming. I explained how frightened I was that he might have hurt me or hurt himself (especially when he was trying to pull the counter top off the island). He spoke openly explaining how angry he was about what was happening to him. He didn't like feeling stupid. He didn't like the constant reminders. He was feeling "less than a man". He felt he had lost control of what was a very calm and caring environment. He didn't like the feel of the medicines. He hated all the doctor appointments. He went on speaking freely for about an hour. By the end of our intervention, Dennis was clearly calming himself and genuinely sorry for the outburst. He didn't understand what had happened. He hugged me and assured me he would never hurt me or let anyone else hurt me -- ever!

On a lighter side, there were the times when comical things would happen. One morning I woke up to find Dennis in a striped sweater -- my striped sweater. He must have gotten cold and put it over his t-shirt. Other times I would be out making breakfast and Dennis would go off to get dressed. He would return with his shorts over his pajama pants. And he would layer two or three shirts on some of the warmest days in Texas.

Shaving became an issue only in that Dennis was meticulous in cleaning the razor after each daily shave. When he came to me saying his razor didn't work, we would just go out to Walmart and buy another. This happened a few times before I realized the problem was he would take the razor apart to clean it -- but he couldn't get it back together correctly with the right parts in place.

The answer to that challenge was simple. Every two weeks, I took him to have a haircut and his beard trimmed. He looked good in a beard so it made everyone happy.

Another unexpected habit reminded me of the little boys' bad habit when they are outside playing and don't want to go in. The last few months when Dennis was home, I noticed he would be going outside to the patio. I just assumed he was going out to play with the dogs. Then one day I looked over to see him go outside but our dogs were inside. I watched to see what he was doing. He walked around to the back of the house and relieved himself by the air conditioner unit. Startled I said, "Denny, what are you doing? You can't go the bathroom outside! Come back in and I will help you to the bathroom." So this continued but under watchful eye. We would see him going out and join him or redirect him by asking if he had to go to the bathroom. His answer was usually yes. It was always ironic and a bit disturbing that to go outside, he had to walk by the guest bathroom. He never did understand my concern, but of course I had to make sure this did not happen when the grandchildren were visiting or out front where the neighbors would see.

Dennis loved going to the mailbox each day. That was his chore and he found pleasure in helping out this way. It worked great until he started spreading out the mail. He would open some envelopes and not others. He would leave some mail on the counter and tuck away others in his drawer or closet. I tried the mail basket in the kitchen. That worked for a bit, but in time going to the mailbox was not feasible. Too many times I didn't get the bills or statements that had due dates or action to be taken. The mail key was taken from its familiar place in the kitchen, and soon he didn't miss that walk to the box.

Daily living with dementia challenges were met with creative ways to make adjustments. I can tell you that many of these events were frustrating to me. In fact, I have to admit I didn't handle things well at times. When I was in denial, I just assumed with a little help he could do much more than he was doing. I thought I could love him out of forgetting or being confused. I wanted to have an answer for everything. It was when I was broken and on bended knee that God spoke clearly to me. Faith, hope and love would have to be my guide. All three were imperative to a meaningful and caring environment for both Dennis and myself.

[What I learned: Make daily life simple. Keep shampoos, soaps and other toiletries to a minimum. There will be times of confusion as to what to use and what to use it for. Keep all medicines securely stored so there is no accidental medication administered. Keep the house orderly and do not rearrange furniture unnecessarily. When you notice clothing selections becoming a problem, keep the selections to a minimum. Encourage a daily routine of personal hygiene to include bathing, brushing teeth and shaving. In our case, shaving became a problem so we went with a beard trim and haircut every two to three weeks.]

Support Groups

Somewhere in those first few weeks after diagnosis, our doctor asked to meet with me privately to go over questions, prognosis and adjustments to be made. In that meeting, he made it clear that Dennis' dementia was caught early and that the life expectancy in this case was about ten years. While those words were ringing in my head, he went on to suggest safety issues at home and the fact that at some point Dennis would not be able to drive. He reminded me how important it was to have the support of our children, family and friends and that facing this was not something to do alone. So with that suggestion, I contacted Alzheimer's Association for available support group opportunities. I was referred to a group that met monthly at a nearby hospital.

Dennis dropped me off at my first meeting and I looked forward to meeting a group of folks who understood the challenges I would face. Much to my disappointment, this group was made up of mostly 70-80 year olds whose spouses had died with Alzheimer's complications. Their experience was far removed from anything I was facing with a 56 year old who was functioning well and in complete denial.

After multiple contacts with the Alzheimer's Association office, I found a support group for Early Stage Alzheimer's. I was assured it would be a way for Dennis and me to network with others who are facing this challenge. We went to that first meeting where spouses and patients were in the same support meeting. Looking around the room we saw nothing but 70+ year olds who were just recently diagnosed. The issues, challenges and questions were not even remotely part of our journey at that point. Folks were talking about the stress on finances. In some cases, couples divorced to avoid loss of their lifetime savings. We both left the meeting knowing this support group did not fit our needs.

At any rate, it only took me a few more visits with various groups to know this was depressing and not helpful for either Dennis or myself. On the other hand, there was a young woman in her late 40's who attended meetings on occasion whose husband had Pick's Disease. That connection with Julie proved to be valuable in the years to come.

In 2003, I made further inquiries and found that there was an Early Onset Alzheimer's chapter in Tulsa, Oklahoma. I became long distance friends with another lady my age whose husband was further along in the disease. We became a good sounding board and support for one another. She put me in touch with her chapter scholarship program and we were invited to their conference.

That conference was difficult for Dennis. He sat through some of the speakers but chose to stay in the hotel room much of the time. For me it was extremely helpful. I learned about the Safe Return program, got tips as a caregiver, and met some of the leading scientists on Alzheimer's out of Bethesda, Maryland.

In a one-on-one conversation after their presentation, I was able to tell our story to the doctors. After hearing the criteria for the diagnosis and medical records, they felt there may just be a bad diagnosis but further testing would be needed. They directed us to the Baylor College of Medicine - Alzheimer's Disease and Memory Care Disorders - for further investigation and research. One particular question they were tackling was "Why do some people get Alzheimer's disease when they are quite young, in their 50s, while others get Alzheimer's disease very late in their lifespan?"

Upon returning, I made the necessary appointments with Dr. Rachelle Doody. We met with her, and she explained the research being done. I was assigned to a Psychologist for Caregivers and Dennis once again met with a Neuropsychiatrist who escorted him to a testing room.

Within a few short minutes, there was a noise in the hallway. It was Dennis' voice! He was yelling that he wanted to leave and "Where is my wife?" I walked out to calm him and assure him of my presence. Before leaving the clinic, I apologized quietly to the staff for the disruption. Upon approaching the elevator, Dennis said he would NEVER agree to any further testing, and I agreed. It was not worth the stress and rage he was feeling.

Unfortunately, I needed the help of that psychologist. I received a call from her, and she explained that I could come for appointments even though Dennis refused to be part of their program. That was the lifeline that I desperately needed at that time. We met on numerous occasions. We discussed the daily challenges, reactions of our children, safety issues, his personal needs, my personal needs, and more. Anything that would give me some relief was fair game. At her suggestion, I journaled and took it to share. I cried and at times she cried. She shared with me that if I wasn't careful, my kids were going to lose two parents. It was evident that I was getting lost in the disease with Dennis. The agony of believing no one understood was more than I could bear at times. It was then that I told her I had an opportunity to go back to work teaching. But my fear was that if I left Dennis, his disease would progress more rapidly. She assured me it would in no way impact the progression of the dementia. What she did advise was that I needed to "find myself" again and she believed teaching was the perfect avenue to accomplish that.

[What I learned: There are numerous support groups in most communities. You will want to visit those and find the place you feel most comfortable. In our immediate area, Interfaith Care Partners (Houston area) sponsored monthly meetings in various churches for those diagnosed and the caregivers. It was a social time for Dennis where he was accepted and could interact with other individuals with dementia. A large group of volunteers would fix a meal and host fun activities. At the same time, caregivers had the morning free or they could meet separately as a support group.]

Recognizing Emotional Limits

We all have different gifts and ways to serve the Lord. Soon after Denny's diagnosis, life began to change in ways other than the element of disease. Individuals I thought were such good friends somehow faded away. Our social network shifted to almost nothing. All I could feel was a loss on all levels of life as I had known it. This shift caused feelings of abandonment, loneliness, sorrow, betrayal and all other feelings that drain you of the positive energy needed to face life under normal circumstances. With that loss and the lack of meaningful support groups, I began to withdraw and focus only on caring for Dennis and whatever was to come.

Staying in the bowels of sorrow is destructive. One evening, I was driving us home from our daughter's. I had been troubled all day by a confrontation/argument we had earlier that morning. With tears falling slowly, I said, "Dennis I am so sorry for the argument this morning. I am not angry at you. I love you! But I hate this damn disease and what it is doing to our lives." Being the godly man that he was and always the comforter, he responded, "Lin, I love you too! But we can't live our lives in anger. We can't look at all the bad stuff. I have lived a good life - a great life. And I will continue to do so as long as God allows. I can swim and bike and we still have each other and our family. It's going to be okay." True to his spirit of the loving and strong husband, his comfort forced me to a new perspective. We never spoke of my sorrow again.

After that conversation, it became perfectly clear to me

that I embrace the help of others who provide a caring and helpful spirit. Angels are not necessarily those that we picture with heavenly wings in the clouds. Not at all, because we soon recognized angels as those who took time to show a caring and supportive spirit. Looking back now, I better understand that we all have the opportunities to assist, help, support and encourage others. Those who recognize the needs of others and so unselfishly give of their time, talents and support are indeed God's warriors.

It is noteworthy to discuss the difference in support from your children. Our son Scott and his family live in Austin, three hours away. With his busy career, business travel and family commitments, we didn't see him much. Scott and his dad shared years of athletic interests, and maintained a strong bond. But as the dementia progressed, he was the one who saw the greatest change mentally, physically and emotionally during his visits. Our daughter Sondra, lived locally and took an active role in supporting her dad's care. She and her oldest son Ian worked with me to keep Dennis engaged in family activities such as birthdays, movies, dinner, swimming, and trips to museums, the zoo and the beach. Her relationship grew stronger as the needs for assistance increased. The point I am making here is how family will determine their level of support based on proximity and levels of emotional ability to do so. Nonetheless, that level of participation should not be seen as a measure of love and concern.

I made a conscious effort to start recognizing the good that was coming to us. I recognized what a blessing it was to have Dennis' best friend Bruce who became a traveling companion and training partner for swimming. I looked at how complete strangers were stepping up to help. As the saying goes, I made it a priority to look at what we had and to forget what was lost.

[What I learned: Recognize your emotional needs. Take care of yourself. Accept your frustrations and your sorrow. For each couple the communication needs and opportunities will be different. Stay connected at some level because your partner's ability to have meaningful conversations will diminish long before you are ready. If not with your loved one, share your sorrows and concerns with someone you trust.]

Angels of Support and Respite

One afternoon, after returning from senior bowling, Dennis said "I met an angel today". I smiled and said, "Really?" He went on to explain that Barb was an angel. She was a neighbor who volunteered to drive him to bowling once a week. And during bowling she helped him when he was confused. He said, "It is like God knows what I need even before I do. So those who help me must be His angels." And from that moment on, we recognized and spoke of our angels.

For me the angels were acquaintances who would stop to ask me about Dennis and how was I doing. Theirs was not a polite passing but a genuine concern and a pause to give a hug. It would be that person who walked past my classroom door and waved just to let me know they were there. And there were neighbors, who in the past, had been just a friendly face but who now called, came by, and helped in any way to show support for the two of us.

For Dennis, the angels were acquaintances who volunteered to take him bowling, drove him to swimming, watched out for him in the neighborhood, sat with him at the hospital, stopped to chat when he wanted to tell his military stories, and engaged him in casual conversation. It was the many volunteers who made him feel welcome at the Gathering Place. It was the high school coach who encouraged him to swim workouts with the high school kids. It was the childhood friend who appeared after 40 years to become his best friend, confidant, voice of reason, traveling companion and co-caregiver. On more than one occasion, it was school district police officers who stepped in during periods of wandering, acting with great support and kindness, helping us get Dennis home safely. And it was my younger brother, Doug, who gave his time and caregiving heart by living with us for the last three years so Dennis had supervision and was safe at home with me.

At this point, I made a commitment to see the good in life, and the people who were readily available to help. This made everything we faced much easier because we were not alone.

Call it what you may, but my reference to angels is because these individuals had no grandiose notion of doing God's work -- it just happened. They unselfishly reached out when they saw a need. The humility of those who cared (sometimes complete strangers) was beyond our daily interactions with our prior circle of support. They were a manifestation of God's perfect timing, comfort and support.

[What I learned: Graciously accept help from others. Recognize a new network of support as it develops in your family, with friends and community. As Dennis said, they were folks who seemed to know what he/we needed even before we did. I read a book during this time, "God Winks" and it helped me recognize the various ways that God makes Himself known in our daily lives. Angels will have no wings and they will have no grandiose ideas of recognition for what they do.]

Changes in the Job

During the next two years that Dennis continued coaching and being Aquatic Coordinator, numerous changes took place in his teaching/coaching assignment.

Because I observed an increase in forgetfulness and time management, I took a more active role in helping Dennis with a calendar of deadlines and detailed paperwork. That extra help seemed to work most of the time. However, at the end of the season when it was time for the swim banquet and awards, Dennis failed to present the awards during the formal dinner. I was unaware this had happened because I did not attend that banquet. I am ashamed to say I was so upset with some parents that I stayed home. When I realized what had happened, I questioned Dennis. I expressed my concern that this would make parents and swimmers upset. He passed it off as not a big deal because he would get it done. When I told our son what had happened, he said, "What worries me most is not that he didn't have awards ready but that he didn't understand that it was important!" At that point I knew I had to be sure he had reminders about even more details than I had originally thought.

For 30 years, Dennis had never had an assistant, but starting that second year of his illness, the district hired a female assistant coach. To be honest, I was initially pleased with this addition of staff. However, the new assistant coach soon took over most everything. Without consulting Dennis, she placed swimmers in their events and planned most of the practice sessions. He expressed his concern that she was not including him in decisions.

Many swimmers no longer saw Dennis as their coach. It wasn't long before Dennis was coming home and puzzled by what was happening and what to do about it. He appreciated the extra help -- in fact, he welcomed it. But it was after all his team for the past 30 years. That program was his "baby". Being the unassuming person that he was, he chose not to cause a conflict or raise questions. He was still doing what he loved - coaching. After a while, he was given assignments like ISC (for students removed from class). Instead of caring for facilities and having travel time, he was locked down to assignments like this that were disturbing to him.

The real hurt began in the fall of 2003 when Dennis was not granted permission to attend the Texas Swim Coaches conference in Austin. The assistant coach traveled to the conference, and Dennis was delegated to stay behind. No reason was given. He had attended that conference for 30 years. When he shared his disappointment and hurt, I knew it was time.

I encouraged him to retire with dignity before something happened and he was asked to leave. I knew it was a delicate situation, even though no one had approached me about difficulties that were observed. All I knew was little by little his role as coach and Aquatic Coordinator had been greatly diminished. He had an incredible history, tenure and reputation with both high school and summer league swimming. I was not about to let him close that career with disgrace or sorrow.

Without Dennis knowing, I met with the Human Resources Director. He was aware of the situation facing

Dennis and the district. We determined Dennis was eligible for full retirement. In addition, he had so much sick time accrued, that it was suggested he start taking that time in January with full pay. He could then schedule theretirement date for the end of that school year in May 2004. This was going to be a win-win situation for the district and for Dennis.

With that information and a full understanding of how the district had a responsibility to the parents and students regarding safety issues, I knew I had to encourage Dennis to retire. In November 2003, I shared with Dennis what I had found out about retirement. I explained what was involved and that we would need to make a trip to Austin for retirement counseling to set everything up. I made it even more inviting because I told him I was going to retire with him. So at that announcement, he was accepting and enthusiastic about us retiring together, and we made that trip to Austin to finalize our retirement plans.

To this day, I am so proud of how our district stood behind Dennis so he could continue working for that short period. I hear horror stories of people being fired and put to the curb. Looking back, I believe they did their best to honor Dennis' years of service while maintaining a safe and orderly environment for students.

[What I learned: Depending on the job responsibilities and the supervising personnel, some effort should be made to determine satisfactory job performance.

Often times, individuals lose more than one job during the progression of dementia. Help your loved one find an acceptable way to continue working or consider opportunities for retirement. It is important that leaving a career or job is planned with dignity honoring years of service if at all possible.]

Sundowning

A few years into the diagnosis, Dennis started having difficulty sleeping. His mother shared with me stories of him sleepwalking as a child. So it was not alarming to me that he demonstrated increased problems sleeping. I was not aware that as many as 20 percent of persons with Alzheimer's experience increased confusion, anxiety and agitation beginning late in the day and through the night. This disruption in the body's sleep-wake cycle soon lead to unexpected behavioral problems.

Swimming and biking were part of Dennis' daily routine. He added to this daily walks of 2-3 miles. He was athletic and his abilities to stay active were what made him feel some quality of life. But the culmination of all that activity contributed to sundowning.

Various medications caused drowsiness, so dozing off during the day was not uncommon. Much like a small child, his biological clock created a mix-up between day and night.

It was not uncommon that periods of sundowning would include opening drawers, doors and turning on lights, arousing me but not necessarily impacting Dennis anymore than sleepwalking. In these situations, I would redirect him to the bathroom or back to bed. I often thought that his wandering was aroused by the urge to go to the bathroom and, on occasion, I was correct.

Serious sundowning manifested itself predominantly after a brief period of sleep. It was as though Dennis became disoriented separating dreams from reality. As this restlessness progressed, he would wake with flashbacks/images of immediate safety threats. He would stand straight up in the bed and scream, "Get up! There are snakes all around us!" At other times, I would wake to find him crawling on the floor as he searched for some unknown object as he murmured nonsensical verbage. Often he was reliving Vietnam memories. Our home was equipped with alarms on the doors and windows, so a door alarm in the middle of the night needed immediate attention. Three exit doors (main, back and garage) required quick checks to make sure he was not outside our fenced/gated yard.

I never woke Dennis unless the sundowning/wandering involved rage and/or was directed at me. As the dementia progressed, Dennis' aggressive and volatile incidents became an increased concern for safety.

Through all of this, I shared the bed with Dennis. Even though there was a temptation at times to use the guest room, I wanted to be with him to avoid any safety concerns. For that reason, I was extremely sleep deprived. It got so bad in the late stages that I went to sleep with a prayer on my lips for my safety/our safety.

[What I learned: With sundowning, it is imperative to keep the environment safe. Secure all medications, knives, and anything that might be used if your loved one

wakes in an aggressive state of mind. Be sure you have some security with the opening and closing of all exterior doors. Avoid nicotine and alcohol, and restrict caffeine consumption to the morning hours and keep evening meals simple. Avoid having visitors in the evening and monitor aggressive and loud television programming. And always keep in mind that your loved one will pick up on your stress and that too can trigger agitation and confusion.]

Driving Concerns

With all that was happening, Dennis would still not accept his diagnosis of Alzheimer's. Even though he took the meds and heard the diagnosis -- denial was his constant companion (and to be honest mine too for about the first five years).

Because of this denial, neither of us were at all concerned about Dennis driving. In fact, in January of 2004, Dennis drove from Houston to Davenport, Iowa to visit his mother. This was a drive he had made numerous times each year starting in 1976. When we talked about it, I had only a tad of concern because I was thinking he might stop for gas then drive off forgetting to pay. He had his cell phone, and I called him or he called me every few hours until he got there. There were no problems! He had a great two-week visit, then drove home without any incidents.

During that next doctor visit, we were so pleased to share the good news of a successful trip. Dennis had done such a remarkable job! We thought our news would please him. WRONG! He looked at me in shock then asked, "You mean to tell me Dennis drove to Iowa alone?" I felt like a child facing certain reprimands from a parent. And so it came.... We were given strict orders to never do that again and how dangerous that could be. The checkup was fine and we left quietly. When we got to the car, Dennis expressed his frustration that the doctor didn't trust him to drive. In our ignorance, neither of us saw the danger.

Another time, I was working as a substitute administrator at an intermediate school. The air conditioning had gone out that day at school. I called Dennis and asked that he please bring me a floor fan. He had driven me to school that morning, and that was a trip he made several times prior. I made that call at about 8:30 am. Noon came and Dennis had not arrived. I could not reach him at home, and he wasn't answering his cell phone. With growing concern, I had friends check other possible places he might be. Then finally I contacted our PISD police department to see if they would check various school facilities to see if he had gone to the wrong school. Nothing! By 6:00 pm, I had no choice but to report him as a missing person. Living in the Houston area with its complex freeway system, I could only imagine he might have taken a wrong turn somewhere and couldn't find his way back.

Time stood still. Friends stopped by the house asking what they could do to help. Others called and told me they were driving the neighborhoods in Pasadena where we had lived for 30+ years, and there was no sighting. 7:00 pm--trying to stay calm; 8:00 pm--friends asking if they can stay with me; 9:00 pm--checked back with police department contact and he had nothing; 10:00 pm --told my friends I was okay and just needed some rest. I laid down to rest and dozed from time to time wondering what possibly happened. I never felt he was in danger, but I thought he was lost for sure. It was 2:00 am the next morning when I got the call. "This is the Brownsville Police Department. We have your husband. We found him at the checkpoint area at the border to Mexico. He is here with us and is okay. He has been very cooperative.

Can you tell me why he was a missing person?" I explained the diagnosis of Alzheimer's. The officer was quite understanding of the urgency at that point. I went on to explain that he had medicines that he had not taken so I wasn't sure what his demeanor might be. I asked if they would please make sure he gets a bite to eat and is comfortable until I got there. I was assured all would be fine. (Later I found out that the information was not passed to the next shift.)

At the end of that call, I immediately called to get the first flight to the Valley so I could drive him home. My trip there provided ample time to think about all that had happened and questions about how he got there. Was he forced to drive someone? I even made a call to his best friend Bruce. We talked through the situation and thought of what to do next. Bruce was quick to suggest that I not jump to any decision about taking Denny's driving privileges away. That was of course heavy on my mind.

I did not arrive at the Brownsville Police Department until after 9:00 am. When I walked in, I was relieved to see Dennis sitting with an officer behind a glass reception area. I walked in to give him a hug. It was more than apparent when I approached him that he was upset ... no he was furious. I asked what was wrong but he didn't get much time to share when the female officer interrupted to say, "Let me tell you what happened!" Dennis kept interrupting and showing me his wrist. He was clearly injured with a swollen wrist. His rage was building. I could hardly hear the officer talking, so they wanted to talk to me privately, but Dennis would have no part of that.

In time, I found out all had gone well through the night. However, at the changing shift in the morning, trouble escalated. Dennis spotted a McDonald's across the street. He told the officers he was going to go get some breakfast. They said he could not leave. He argued that he wasn't arrested and had done nothing wrong. He tried to leave against their orders, and that was when a struggle occurred. Dennis fought back from being restrained and during his rage, his wrist was inadvertently injured.

With all this conversation going on, Dennis' level of rage was building once again. He stormed down the hall of the holding area and tried to break through the door. The entire time he is screaming, "I am getting the hell out of here!" I did my best to stay with him and calm him. As chaos continued, numerous officers appeared behind me. I kept pleading with him to please calm down so we could go home. I confirmed with him that we could not leave until he calmed down. This negotiation was interrupted by a voice behind me. It was a female officer who spoke in a soft tone. She said, "Dennis, we are so sorry for what has happened to you. This whole thing should have been handled differently. Please accept our apology. If you just listen to your wife, she is here to take you home."

Her kindness seemed to console his rage enough that I could sign the necessary documents and take Dennis safely to the car. He was hungry, so I took him for breakfast. On the drive back to Houston, Dennis continued to tell his story. He pleaded with me he did nothing wrong. He didn't understand what all the fuss was about. His rage built once again when he relived the injury to his wrist. He slammed his fist on the dash of the van while I was driving. Up to then, I let him vent. At that point I had to put a stop to some of it. I said, "You have got to stop the rage! It is dangerous for me to drive like this. If you don't stop, I will not be able to drive us safely home".

After a doctor visit soon thereafter, we knew that Dennis' injury was superficial and the swelling would subside in time. Sometime during the next week, an officer from the Brownsville Police Department called to make sure Dennis was okay. She apologized once again on behalf of the department regarding how the incident was handled.

Relieved that Dennis was home safely, the driving issue had to be addressed. I couldn't ignore what had happened. For one thing Adult Protective Services contacted me as part of their investigation as a result of the missing person report on an Alzheimer's family member.

A concerned neighbor called me one day and said she had told her computer technician about Denny's story and all that was happening. He had shared with her that he could put a tracking device on our vehicles so that would not happen again. Being a skeptic, I listened and decided to at least talk with the young man. We met and he explained that I would need an account with Accutracking and a T-mobile phone to do this. The phones would be hard-wired into the vehicles and this would allow me to get on the computer at any time and see where our vehicles were located. The good news with this was that I didn't have to involve police officers, and he couldn't get too far away without us finding him.

With an investment of a few hundred dollars, I had the system installed on both our vehicles. It was incredible! I could actually see the car sitting in the lot or driveway. I didn't say anything to Dennis because I knew he would not like the idea, but he was definitely NOT ready to stop driving, so this was my safety net.

And so the story goes .... we had a few more incidents where he got lost, and with the help of the technician and a few friends in the PISD police department, we could always find him and get him safely home. While being observed by myself and officers, Dennis could clearly drive with care and follow the laws of safety. His problem was wandering and getting lost.

One day I returned home from work to find Dennis on the driveway. He had components of the tracking device all torn out of his vehicle. He was furious! He said, "What the hell is this? Don't you trust me?" In frustration I came back at him with, "Of course I do! I am just doing everything I can to let you drive safely. I am the only one who thinks you should still be driving. I am on your side but I have to answer to the law and others regarding how I am keeping you safe. Now you have just ruined that for yourself."

Later that evening, when we had both calmed down, we talked about the tracking system. I assured Dennis I was trying to make sure he had the freedom to live a quality life. I continued to emphasize my commitment to being on his side. He apologized and told me, "You are the only one who really understands me. I don't know where I would be without you." We spoke of our faith and how it was important to take things just one day at a time.

My technician installed the equipment so Dennis could continue to drive a vehicle, but as you can guess, the issues later became safety for others, and not just his wandering. Timing for taking away driving privileges is crucial to everyone. But most important-- thought and consideration for the safety of everyone should be part of the plan. Dennis was a caring person who would never want to hurt another person. When we were together, I did all the driving. While I was at work, I arranged transportation for Dennis so he could swim and bowl. The process was never an abrupt halt. It was gradual and uneventful in the process of change.

[What I learned: Adult Protective Services are social services that investigate abused, neglected, or exploited older adults and adults with significant disabilities. If police or hospital staff report any concerns, you will be investigated. There are questions that must be answered to give assurance your loved one is being properly supervised.]

Cycling Challenges

Dennis had been an avid cyclist for almost 30 years. When we lived in Pasadena, he left the house each morning at 5:00 to peddle his way to the high school about 10+ miles away. As a coach, he was trying to find time for a personal workout, so this was his uncompromised time to take care of that.

Cycling was relaxing for him. I remember when Scott was getting ready to leave for college, we went out shopping for a new bike. Dennis' bike had problems and we just decided to purchase another more updated one. Off we went to the Bike Barn. He rode a Schwinn mountain bike and loved it. Much to my surprise he said, "Lin, I want you to try one of these bikes for yourself." I fussed and said that was a waste for me, but he insisted. After a brief test ride, we found ourselves the proud new owners of two new bikes. And for a period of about five years, we would have our carefree bike rides through the neighborhoods and on the bike paths of Iowa during the summer.

Dennis had mentioned for several years that he would love to do the RAGBRAI, an annual 400+ mile bike ride across Iowa. He had read about it -- and just wanted to do it someday. In 2006, four years after the diagnosis, I made contact with the Davenport bike club about how to get Dennis registered for the ride. There was a lottery and you couldn't just automatically register to go. They gave me further contacts as I shared our story of Alzheimer's. I knew it had to be sooner rather than later for him to be able to make this ride. Before the initial registration,

I spoke with our son Scott, also an avid cyclist. I asked him to join his dad for the ride. I knew it would create great memories for the two of them, but just as important was the constant supervision for this 444 mile, week long event. Of course he was on board to make this dream of his dad's possible.

In Texas Dennis started training in January, for the ride. He increased his daily mileage and added the conditioning of continued distance swimming. When we got to Iowa in early June, Steve (Dennis' brother and cyclist) took

Dennis Shippey with son Scott (on left)

on the responsibility of more intense training with long distance rides several times a week. Watching Steve and Dennis ride off for their morning rides each day was so heartwarming. This was truly a team effort. His brother's attention to training and conditioning kept Dennis focused and inspired. As the time approached, his increased excitement and enthusiasm was noticeable to everyone. Afternoon naps were part of the daily routine but it was all good -- and obvious to everyone that he could physically make the ride.

Steve and I had some concerns about Dennis' bike. This was after all, a 444 mile ride up and down hills. He had noticed that Denny was needing some reminders to shift on the hills to preserve his energy. We visited the local Sparky's bike shop and found a terrific buy on a Klein road bike. It was a gem! Dennis thought he had a Cadillac. He was like a little kid who wanted to sleep with his new toy. We threw in some 'Butt Butter' and a few other necessities as final preparation for the trip. He moved his odometer from the older bike and he was ready to continue training for the 'ride of a lifetime'.

Scott and I had discussed the logistics of camping each night, and the backup support that would make this ride possible. At the time, we owned a van, and I would follow the route at a distance or ahead as a support vehicle. There were many unknowns to be covered: sleeping in a different place every night, sleeping in a tent, night wandering, getting to portable potties in the middle of the night, then finding his way back and so on. Scott very carefully placed his tent close to his dad's so he would know if there was movement. Of course his dad's snoring didn't make things pleasant, but it was a sacrifice for safety.

At each stop for the day, we would meet. I would hear the stories of their day and the warm hospitality of all the wonderful people along the way. There were laughs and detailed stories of sites seen along the ride. All in all, the ride was a great success. And we (Scott, Steve and myself) felt like we had been a part of something very special. Together we made it possible for Dennis to fulfill this dream.

After the ride, it wasn't long before Dennis was unable

to ride out on the roads with a group. His inability to follow cycling etiquette made it dangerous for him to be in a group (for himself and others). He no longer had the automatic timing to change gears to ride altering terrains. At that point Dennis was limited to riding in our neighborhood for short rides that were monitored.

On a hot summer day, he left for a ride in the morning and did not return at his regular time. Hours passed and neighbors helped me check surrounding neighborhoods to see if we could find him. Nothing! It was 100 degrees by early afternoon and I grew increasingly concerned. Finally I had no choice. I had to notify police so they would also be on the alert. An officer came to our house to take the report. I provided a current photo and the needed information to put things in motion. Late in the afternoon the officer returned to speak with me. As we were talking Dennis rode up on his bike. He was hot, exhausted and irritated to see the officer there. We tried to speak with him but he was doing his best to disregard our concerns. He went on to explain he didn't see the problem or why the officer was there. He told the officer, "I was over by the freeway waiting for her because she said she was picking me up. When she didn't come, I just found my way back home". With that he walked into the house. I thanked the officer and apologized and explained there was no agreement that I would pick him up.

During his next visit to our house, Scott promptly flattened both tires on the bike. He said under no circumstances should his dad be riding, and soon thereafter we sold the bike. It was a subtle transition that caused no anguish for Dennis.

[What I learned from this: It is important to keep your loved one engaged with familiar activities and with loved ones other than yourself.   That person needs to feel as "normal" as possible in this downward ability to relate to their environment. The doctors will confirm that supervision and familiar activities will help your loved one emotionally and physically. Find family members or friends who are willing to get involved. Equally important is that the person supervising your loved one have a current picture, list of medications and doctor contact.]

The Hurricane

Living on the Gulf Coast, hurricanes are a familiar concern. Having lived in the Houston area, we had never evacuated for tropical storms or threat of hurricanes. We just hunkered down and prepared with all safety precautions in place.

Dennis was actually doing well in 2005. We were three years into the diagnosis of Alzheimer's and with small adjustments we were doing well. But when reports of an oncoming hurricane were being predicted, our daughter Sondra insisted that we join her family in an evacuation journey. Sadly, millions of other people in the Houston area had the same idea. We were driving a caravan of three vehicles with a baby, a toddler, three dogs and a cat when we met up with gridlock on the freeway. The temperature was hovering at about 100+ degrees. We determined it best to take the toll road thinking that would be a better route. What we found was bumper-to-bumper vehicles traveling north from Houston at a speed of about 10-15 mph.

Our destination was Austin. The trip from Houston to Austin would normally have taken three hours, but in that instance it took almost 24 hours. It was one of the most frightening things I have ever experienced. Gas was not readily available so when you did find a station, the lines were miles long. Restrooms along the way were even more scarce. Small necessities that make a trip normal were all but gone. What we quickly learned was to turn off the air conditioner, and when moving at that slow pace you would preserve gas. Since we left the house late in the afternoon, we welcomed sundown in this dastardly heat. Even in the heat of the night, temperatures were soaring such that we had washcloths to wipe the foreheads and faces of the little ones and just enough water to keep the animals hydrated.

Three years later, weather advisors were predicting another hurricane. This one was predicted to hit the Galveston area. Since I already knew that we would not evacuate, we got busy preparing the house for the possibility of a few days with no electricity. In addition, Dennis and I worked diligently to clear the yard of any objects that could fly in the high winds only to cause unnecessary damage. We planned for the worst case scenario where we would take a direct hit, and stored supplies in a big walk-in closet. Even though Dennis knew what we were doing, it was now 2008 and he didn't seem to be concerned with any of the dangers. He just did his best to help with tasks as I presented them to him.

September 16, 2008, Hurricane Ike slammed into the Gulf Coast, shredding buildings, flooding streets, and knocking out power for millions of people. With winds reaching 110 miles an hour, Ike came ashore over Galveston, Texas, as a strong Category 2 storm just after 3:00 am. The massive storm, nearly as big as Texas itself, moved over Houston before dawn.

The high powered winds hit before the eye of the storm. It was nighttime and we lost all power. Dennis and I just laid down to try and rest. My goal was to keep him calm as the storm passed over. About 2:00 am we heard a loud blast of breaking glass. I ran to the living area to see the window had exploded. The closed blinds kept the flying glass from doing much damage, but the heavy rains were pummeling our living room. Normally, Dennis would have taken charge and I would have assisted. Yet now, I saw his look of confusion. He was at a loss. With only a flashlight, I headed for the garage. I remembered seeing a window-sized piece of plywood by the cabinet. My only thought was to see if that piece of plywood would cover the area and keep the rain from pouring in. Dennis followed me running back and forth. He expressed concern, "What is going on?" I asked him to just stay with me and we would be okay. After seeing that the plywood covered the opening, I had to find a way to anchor it in place. The winds were blowing extremely hard, so the blinds were not holding back anything. We moved furniture and I took hammer/nail to pound the wood and the blinds to the wall.

With a sigh of relief, we moved back to the bedroom. Dennis needed to use the bathroom, but when we walked into the master bath there was water on the floor. In the dark, I couldn't figure out where it was coming from. No broken windows were evident, but while I was mopping it up I felt a drip. The water was streaming in the ceiling vent. There was a ceiling fan and vent in close proximity, and both were providing a pathway for a steady stream of water. After laying a pathway of towels to the commode, Dennis was safe to take care of business.

With water coming in the den window, water dripping from the bathroom ceiling, and later water coming in the kitchen ceiling, we were finally at a point where we went back to lie down and wait out the storm. Once we were settled, Dennis seemed to calm like a child cuddled with parents during a storm. I laid there wondering what we would wake up to at dawn and how to possibly handle the damages without the help of my husband. I knew he would not be the handyman who could help put things back together. I had a challenge coming my way.

When the sun rose and the winds calmed, we looked outside to see our backyard carpeted with black and silver shingles from our neighbor's house. Their shingles had most likely acted as torpedos, breaking our windows. There were trees torn out by their roots, and foreign objects in the yard and flower beds. Once outside, we saw our roof had received heavy damage with large areas of missing shingles. There were no broken windows in the kitchen area but there was a substantial leak across the ceiling. All in all, we were okay and the property damage would be repaired.

Scott called early that morning and asked how he could help. I explained the situation and we decided we would bring supplies from Austin for both us and our daughter Sondra. He brought two huge generators, large gas cans full of gas, extra long heavy duty extension cords and heavy duty trash bags for clean up. It was a welcome site when he arrived. Dennis was so happy to see him and did what he could to unload the truck.

Our insurance company suggested we move out of the house while repairs were made. I explained that was not in Dennis' best interest. He was familiar with our home, and I didn't want things to be any worse than they already were by taking him to a strange place to live. A quick call to my brother Doug in Iowa got us some much needed help to supervise repairs and keep Dennis comfortable.

With all the confusion and destruction, I praised God for my brother who was able to help when I returned to work. And what a blessing it was to have an insurance company that understood the importance of keeping Dennis in his familiar surroundings. There is no doubt in my mind, extra effort was made to get things done because of the challenges of Alzheimer's. After all was said and done, we had much to be thankful for.

[What I learned from this: Anything that disrupts the normal routine of living can be a challenge. In this case an approaching hurricane, evacuation, extreme heat and a home in disarray were all very stressful for my husband. Keep in mind the environment must remain as constant as possible. The familiar is a necessary part of keeping confusion to a minimum.]

Long Hospital Stay

It was early in June 2009 when I woke to find Dennis on the floor doubled-up in pain. He could not get up. I knew I needed help moving him, so I hurried to the phone to see if a neighbor could come. By the time our neighbor arrived, I knew I had to get Dennis to the hospital. This pain was beyond anything that I had seen him experience in the past.

When we got to the emergency room, tests were run and nothing was found to be a problem. It was a puzzle. He was admitted for observation and further testing. He had to have a CT Scan with contrast or ultrasound or both, I can't remember which. When he was returned to the room, we sat quietly until the doctor could come in to talk with us. Within no more than 15 minutes after everyone left the room, Dennis went into respiratory arrest. I called for help immediately, and everyone came rushing in.

I was escorted to the hallway while the nurses and staff worked feverishly to get Dennis back. When they were able to revive him he was moved to Intensive Care. While in the ICU, Dennis was on a ventilator for three days. We weren't getting much information as to the cause and what all was happening. Our doctor said that a medication they gave him, when combined with the Alzheimer's drugs, caused respiratory arrest. It was a medication Dennis obviously could not tolerate.

During those three days, our kids and friends kept vigil with me. I contacted our parish priest to see if he could come to visit the hospital. He was out of town but assured me he would see us when he returned. Those days were emotionally draining. The kids dealt with things differently as would be expected -- and of course, I was in a deep fog. Things were said. Feelings were hurt. The kids weren't speaking to one another. Then the door opened and in came Father James. We were all by Dennis' bedside with deep confusion, fright and sorrow. Father did an incredible job of bringing us together as a family. In prayer, we were able to once again focus on Dennis' health crisis. The church no longer calls it Last Rites but instead calls this prayer visit, the Anointing of the Sick. When Dennis came off the ventilator and was able to speak with us, he said he remembered nothing about what had happened. On the fourth day, Dennis came out of ICU and spent a few days in this acute care hospital before being transferred to a long term care hospital for a month of IV therapy.

Once transferred to the long term care facility, our real challenges began. Dennis had developed extensive blood clots in both calves that now caused concern. The doctor ordered an IVC filter to be placed in his abdomen. Because he was not a candidate for coumadin, or other blood thinners, the filter insured that dangerous blood clots would not travel to the heart or brain.

Our doctor had determined that it was the movement of a blood clot to Dennis' abdomen that caused the original pain the morning I found him on the floor. Through IV therapy, it was believed he would regain his strength and be able to return home. That treatment period was about four and a half weeks. An Alzheimer's patient in the hospital is a caregiver's worst nightmare. The very day we transferred Dennis, I saw that he was being put in a room a good distance from the nurse's station. I got into a heated discussion with the admitting nurse stating this was not going to be a good situation because of Dennis' wandering during the night. This was a new and strange environment so I anticipated his confusion to increase (especially since the doctor was not continuing all the Alzheimer's drugs for that period of time). Once the nurse saw I was not going to back down from the battle, she took me aside and said, "Please let your doctor know that he should order a one-on-one care attendant for 24 hours a day." She explained she was not supposed to tell me that, but she understood my concerns, and after a brief time with Dennis, she agreed.

Even with the care attendant, I spent countless hours at the hospital. At night I tried to get some rest only to be called at 1:00, 2:00, and 3:00 in the morning by the charge nurse. There were concerns ranging from him wandering into people's rooms, to being combative, to taking apart his bedding and so on. There was medication they could give him, but it had not been on the orders, so I would travel to the hospital with the medicines hidden in my purse. Once I would get Dennis settled, I would return home making sure I let the doctor know that those meds must be ordered (PRN as needed). Their calls were always a plea for help. "We can't do anything with him." "He won't listen." "He wants to go home." " He is looking for you!" Looking back I can only relate this experience to that of a child looking for the parent. Hospitalization was frightening for Dennis when I was not by his side.

Dennis responded well to the IV therapy and physical therapy such that after four and a half weeks, I was able to bring him home. It was such a relief, and we were both excited to be back home together. Dennis was weak but was cognitively doing well and was in good spirits.

Three days later, the pain returned. I called the doctor, and he said for me to take Dennis back to the hospital immediately. This time a big part of the pain was kidney failure. Once admitted, it was determined that his kidneys were working only at about 15% capacity. The urologist gave me little hope that this would be reversed without dialysis and the treatment plan was started immediately. During those days, the nurses cautioned me that this may be the "beginning of the end". I started thinking of hospice and the decisions that would have to be made. I was in a whirlwind of emotion trying to take it all in and do the right thing for Dennis. When our regular doctor arrived, he said his office was getting calls about hospice. He asked, "Have you given up"? I explained the conversations with nurses and hospital staff. He assured me he thought Dennis would pull through and that he wouldn't give up if I didn't.

My heart filled with joy as once again Dennis was transferred to the long term care hospital. His kidneys responded remarkably well to the treatment but he had infection in the lungs that needed IV therapy once again. It was another four and a half weeks of treatment before we came home. We continued with a one-on-one care attendant, but the daily changing of personnel who had little experience with caregiving for dementia patients continued to cause issues for Dennis.

When we were finally able to go home, Dennis was extremely weak. My brother, Doug, came to live with us to help out. He and Dennis would take little walks at first and eventually worked up to walking the one-mile path around our community lake. He resumed his bowling once a week and was actively involved with Doug ... attending Gatherings for individuals with dementia.

During this last stay in the hospital, there was one day when I came to visit him and it was relatively quiet. I was sitting next to the windows where we had placed 10-15 family pictures. Dennis was glancing past me to a picture when he said, "If you stay for just a little while, you will meet Linda. She is my wife, and you will really like her." I was taken aback until I looked at the picture and realized it was a younger picture of me. In that moment, I realized he didn't recognize me but did recognize the picture. I just took a deep breath and assured him I would stay, and that I would love to meet her. Then we went on about our morning routine.

What I learned from all this hospitalization time was that the family must speak loudly to maintain proper care for their loved ones. Stay with them as much as possible, and when that's not possible make sure proper supervision is in place. In Dennis' case, I had to give a voice for his needs and be an advocate to educate all those who worked with him regarding his family, his interests and various ways to engage him in conversation. I made a booklet that provided all care attendants and visitors with a background of experiences that would help them connect with Dennis. I was amazed how many people commented on how much they learned from that booklet.

Beyond the physical and emotional challenges faced during these hospital stays, I became alarmingly aware of how poorly staffed hospitals are when caring for dementia patients. I vowed to never forget the experiences we had and to somehow do what I could to draw awareness to the needs for the hospital and the families in this situation.

What I learned: Hospitals are ill-equipped to supervise dementia patients that are mobile. Work with the staff administrators and hospital social workers to make sure you know what can be provided so you can get rest. Hospital visits are disorienting under the best of conditions. For the dementia challenged, it is a nightmare of obstacles and unfamiliar people who are in and out of the room with little or no information about the patient.]

Missing Person: The Lucky Bark

February 5, 2009, Dennis took our grandson's dog, Lucky, for a walk at a nearby park. He was visiting at our daughter's home in Pasadena where we had lived for almost 30 years and took the old familiar walk to the park or around the block. Lucky and Dennis were buddies. It was their routine anytime he was there for a visit.

It was also Dennis' birthday. I was teaching at the time at a nearby high school. We had plans to go to dinner to celebrate another great year. About 4:00 pm, I arrived to pick Dennis up. A family friend had been with Dennis all day, and he said he was concerned that Dennis had not returned yet from his walk. So off I went driving to the park and around the block to see if I could catch up with him.

When I didn't find him in the immediate vicinity, I called nearby friends and our daughter to help in the search. Within 30 minutes or less, I knew we needed help. While still searching, I called 911. The operator asked a few questions that annoyed me because all I wanted was help. Then I got the message - "You will have to hang up and call your local police department. This is not an emergency for 911." At that I got more than a little hostile. I kept calling back to no avail.

Following her directive, I had to abandon my search and go back to the house to get the number for the local police department. I knew by then we were facing a potentially dangerous situation. Contacting the police department was another frustration. To be quite honest, being transferred from one person to another (each asking what were my needs) made my blood boil. Finally, I was told that an officer would be dispatched to the house to take an official report and get the detailed information.

I waited about 45 minutes as daylight slipped away. At 7:30 pm, the officer finally arrived. My immediate concern was to have everyone on the alert to watch for Dennis and Lucky. The questioning seemed endless. There were the obvious questions: height, weight, what was he wearing, his address, birthdate, description of the dog, dog's name. Asking about parent information, social security, where he was born, and so on seemed utterly ridiculous. All this was being scribed into a little spiral notebook with no sense of urgency. My anxiety was impossible to contain. I kept pleading for quick response for officers on patrol to have this information. I explained that we had about six family/friends looking and where we had looked. When the officer left, I felt some relief that FINALLY we had our help.

About 10:00 pm we got a call. An officer had located Dennis. We were all so excited and everyone withdrew the search. They would be bringing Dennis home within the hour. Thirty minutes later the phone rang. It was not the call we wanted. There had been a mistake. The individual they had stopped was NOT Dennis after all.

I had no choice but to stay by the phone. I went to our home in Pearland to stay that night thinking he might have walked the ten miles home and showed up there. But there were no phone calls and no Dennis.

With the help of her friend, Sondra made flyers with pictures of her dad and that he was missing. They did a great job. She spent the night driving the streets and talking with anyone who was open for business. She explained the urgency of finding her father and left them with a flyer that provided contact numbers. When dawn came she passed a patrol car and decided to stop and share the flyers with the officers. As she told her story of searching and provided the flyers, she was shocked and horrified that they knew nothing of the search. By then in was 8:00 am, and Dennis had been missing 16 hours.

The officers were apologetic and suggested she contact Texas EquuSearch. They gave her the contact number and assured her they would provide the help we needed. Sondra called me with this information and told me what the officers advised. At first I was reluctant, but we were desperate for help.

I promptly called the contact number and found an immediate response to our cry for help. They took the case number for my report to law enforcement and said they would set up a command station at the park where Dennis had last been seen. They were never hesitant to help. They had only one request and that was for me to contact the supervising officer in charge of the investigation to let him know they were joining the search. It was a protocol that they honored to keep everyone informed and working together. I was assured the search personnel would be on site in a couple of hours.

While I was contacting EquuSearch, Sondra had contacted her office at the Water Department. All city employees had been given the information and were keeping their eyes open as they went about their daily duties. The school district police department was doing the same. So at that point we had pretty much canvassed the Pasadena area.

In relaying this new support status to the local police department, I expressed my frustration and utter disgust that the officers on the street that morning knew nothing. The officer apologized and said he would look into that and get back with me.

In a return call, I was told that there had been a computer glitch and that the report had not been put out on the network but that had been corrected. I was also advised that detectives would be meeting me within the hour at our daughter's home.

When the two detectives arrived, I did not feel any sense of urgency on their part. They asked what I thought were mundane and stupid questions. What I wanted was ACTION. I wanted reassurance that people were looking for my husband. This was February and he had been missing 18 hours. The detectives asked if they could search the house and our vehicles. My response was one of fury. I had no kind words at that point.

Luckily for me, friends and fellow PISD police officers were with me for support, and they advised me to let the detectives do their job. Later I realized the detectives didn't appreciate the presence of the district officers, but they were my friends and were there only for support.

While all this was happening, our son Scott arrived from Austin to join the search. His immediate concern was to calm me down as I vented about the searching of the home and vehicles. He knew calm was what was needed to get the job done.

When the search was finished I provided Dennis' doctor's information to confirm the Alzheimer's. I asked for an immediate Silver Alert posting. Much to my disbelief, I was told Dennis did not qualify for the Silver Alert because he was not yet 65. I argued to no avail and expressed my fury that his diagnosis at age 64 would not be considered.

Then one of the detectives asked me to speak with him in his vehicle. His line of questioning did nothing but infuriate me. He and I had some terse words, and I left the vehicle. He asked to speak with the person who last saw Dennis. It was Craig, a family friend, who had been with him all day. By this point, Craig was an absolute wreck. He loved Dennis like a brother. He was distraught thinking over what he might have done differently. The detective took him to that same vehicle. Craig returned from that interrogation visibly distressed. He said they wanted him to go with them for a lie detector test, but he was having no part of it. Already frustrated with the detectives, I expressed my opinion and supported Craig categorizing the request as absolute nonsense and a waste of time. I did, however, offer to provide them with the Accutracking report for the van they had used that day. It would give detailed locations and times for all the time in question. They didn't request it, but I gave it to them anyway.

The detectives were at the house for a couple of hours. Shortly after they left, we got the call that EquuSearch was starting to set up their command post at the park. It was early afternoon now and still no sign of Dennis. I remember sitting on a park bench that day with a good friend. I had calmed in the tranquility of the park. Total strangers continued arriving; families, volunteers, friends of friends. All I could think of was how awesome it was to finally have this abundance of help (now almost 20 hours later). Everyone drove by as they reported to the command station and got their assignment. Even though Scott and Sondra were in and out of that area, I purposely stayed away from the hub because the overabundance of energy would have only taken me to a more fearful place in my heart and mind.

People were coming and going all afternoon and early evening. The television stations were alerting the community about Dennis' disappearance. Our daughter worked for the city water department and her superintendent had all employees on alert for any possible sighting. The school district police department had all officers alerted to the disappearance so they could join the search.

Friends and strangers came by to give me a hug and provide support. At about 8:00 pm, Scott, Sondra and I went to the command station to thank everyone. Among the search coordinators on site were the two detectives and my friends from the PISD police department. It was quieting down as the coordinator had started sending volunteers home for the night. He explained to me that at 9:00 pm the search would be suspended till early morning. At that point, we all needed to try to get some rest.

At the crack of dawn, we were all back at the park. People were coming and going on that chilly morning. I remember thinking that Dennis had been missing two consecutive nights in the cold of February. I could only pray he found a warm place to sleep. I found myself in constant prayer. Only the Lord could carry me through these hours of desperation.

At 10:00 am that Saturday morning, the kids came running to me on the park bench. They had found Dennis! He was in an Angleton, Texas hospital. Hunters found him in a field 45 miles from where the walk began! The search was officially over!

Scott, Sondra, our grandson Ian and I jumped in a vehicle to make the trip. We had no detailed information but that he was alive and in the hospital emergency room. When we arrived in the emergency room, Dennis looked absolutely weathered and disoriented. He smiled and was clearly pleased to see family. His heart rate was extremely high. He was dehydrated. Doctors said he was near death when he came in. He was stable at that point so they were moving him to Intensive Care.

On our way to the hospital, a trooper had called to let me know he had Lucky. The dog was okay and he would bring him to me at the hospital. When the trooper arrived with Lucky, we got more information. He said two young men were out hunting rabbits that morning in a nearby thicket and heard a dog barking. It was a strange bark

81

and not one that they expected to hear in the middle of nowhere. When they found the dog, they saw that he was tied to a small tree. They also noticed a pile of clothes on the ground but no one was nearby. As they stood wondering what to do, they heard a sound. They looked out to see Dennis standing in the middle of the thicket mumbling incomprehensible sounds. They immediately called 911. The trooper went on to describe how difficult it was to get back into that area with paramedics. I could only cry out, "Thank you Jesus". When I asked for the names of the hunters so I could give them a cash reward, the trooper said everyone was so focused on caring for Dennis that they never got the names.

After turning over Lucky to us, I asked the trooper if we could speak privately. I asked if he felt Dennis had been abducted and driven there? Had he been physically or sexually abused? The trooper said that was one of the first things they looked for. After careful examination, the medical staff truly believed that Dennis had walked that distance on his own. There was no indication of foul play.

When I share this story with friends, they all say, "You aren't suppose to know their names. They were angels sent to save Dennis' life." And so I title this post, the Lucky Bark. Lucky stayed with Dennis and inevitably saved his life. Without that bark, Dennis may have breathed his last breath in the middle of nowhere. He may never have been found.

Once Dennis was admitted to Intensive Care, we contacted our family doctor. He requested that Dennis be transported back to our local hospital. Dennis was transported by ambulance to Pasadena the next day. In Bayshore hospital, it soon became apparent that they did not have the staffing to supervise him. Our doctor cleared any health concerns and released him to me for home care and recovery. I was better equipped to keep him in a safe and familiar environment.

[What I learned: Plan ahead for possible emergencies. Have contact numbers readily available if your loved one wanders. Post the phone number for your local police department and your doctor near a phone or program to cell phone. Even with a safe and secure home environment, supervising your loved one is an important part of caregiving. Whether it is something as simple as a walk, a bike ride or a swim, having a companion is important. Keep hospital stays to a minimum if home care can be provided. And understand that anytime police are involved with wandering, you will be contacted by Adult Protective Services.]

Adult Protective Services

Before being discharged from the hospital there was a legal issue that emerged. As a result of Dennis being reported a missing person, Adult Protective Services would had a social worker representative interview Dennis and me regarding safety. Having already been investigated by APS after the Brownsville incident, I knew the routine. And after such a blatantly poor response by the law enforcement regarding the 911 call, I was defensive and not in the mood for another interrogation by anyone.

When the lady started the all too familiar questioning, I politely interrupted and explained the safeguards that were in place. I told her, "We have made the necessary adjustments on this journey with Alzheimer's". She stopped me in that sentence to correct me by noting this was not a journey. Then she had me -- how dare she correct me. I proceeded to tell her this was my life, and it was a journey. I knew what she was going to ask, so I saved her time.

"I have put in place many safeguards. I have a tracking device on all vehicles. I have a care attendant who stays with Dennis daily while I work. I have him registered with the national Safe Return program. And I am working with a psychologist who specializes in caring for Dennis and myself during this time. He no longer drives, so that is not a problem. It has been and always will be my intention to let Dennis live life to it's fullest with necessary safeguards. He had walked the dog on a regular basis and in a familiar neighborhood many times with no problem. Have I missed anything? Have I answered all your questions?" At that, she closed her notebook and acknowledged, "I am just doing my job and it is obvious you are doing yours. I wish all my cases were this simple. Good luck to you!" She knew at that point there was no neglect and/or abuse in this case.

It was absolutely amazing. Near death experience with only three days hospitalization and he was going home. He didn't remember much about the period of time when he was missing other than to say the dog got tired and he carried him. He also said that when sleeping at night, he piled up leaves and stuff to make himself a bed.

[What I learned: Adult Protective Services are advocates for adults who are vulnerable with physical or mental challenges. Their role is on the same line as Child Protective Services. Just know they will contact you and they will most likely visit your home for an interview with your loved one and yourself. They will make sure your home is safe and you are taking appropriate measures to maintain adequate medical care. Be prepared with detailed information regarding medical care that includes doctor visits and prescribed medications. Give them the names and contact information of all individuals who supervise or help supervise your loved one 24 hours a day. Explain to them the safeguards you have taken in your home to insure safety at all times. Discuss any activities that are regularly scheduled outside the home. And above all, keep a binder of all documents that can support your ability to protect and care for your loved one.]

Visting Law Enforcement

A week after getting Dennis home, I made an appointment with the local chief of police. I met with him to thank the department for support. And as an educator, I wanted to share with him some of my concerns about the investigation and how it could very well have cost my husband his life.

Unfortunately, I was a woman alone. My gesture to provide suggestions and ask serious questions was met with great resistance. It was clear this department accepted no responsibility for failing to broadcast the missing person alert until almost 15 hours later.

Not being fully satisfied with that meeting with the chief, I went on to meet with the mayor. I wanted to discuss my concerns about the handling of the 911 call and the delayed reporting to patrol vehicles. He had obviously been forewarned of my issues. He politely listened and it was more than apparent he would NOT be doing anything further after I left. He politely brushed the case off as a failure that had been addressed.

That summer Dennis and I were visiting family in Iowa. My brother had told me about their local program called Project Lifesaver. PL was a program that provided timely response to save lives for children and adults who wander due to Alzheimer's, autism, and other related disorders. I used the contact information and set up the initial registration and interview to register Dennis. Before we met with the liaison officer, I talked with Dennis about this program. He was not fond of the idea and didn't want to participate. But when I explained the freedom it would give him and how it protected both of us, he agreed to participate. We completed all requirements and they provided Dennis with the wrist transmitter that was secured with a special lock. Even though it was never needed during that visit, it was a meaningful safety net. It was sad to know at the end of our visit, we would have to turn in the beacon.

Without something like Project Lifesaver, searches can involve multiple agencies, hundreds of officers, countless man hours and thousands of dollars. Not only that, time is critical when someone wanders and can lead to a tragic outcome.

Without hesitation, I went back to my Texas home on a mission to find this program. It did not exist and there was nothing comparable. I began to research the program to see what I could do to present this opportunity to our local law enforcement.

Without going into great detail, I found that there was a $4000 cost for startup. It would mean training a team of officers and equipment. I contacted the Texas representative for Project Lifesaver and asked him to attend a scheduled meeting with the Harris County Sheriff Administration team and me. I presented the material, and the representative answered all questions. I offered to personally pay the $4000 and coordinate volunteers for the registration process. They listened politely, then told me they appreciated the information but Harris County was too big an area for this program. I suggested that they consider just setting it up in my precinct as a pilot, to see if it would be effective for our large community. Nothing was accepted, and I left completely frustrated. Frustrated, yes, but filled with satisfaction that I had given a voice to other families and individuals facing the challenges of Alzheimer's, and for now that had to be enough.

[What I learned from this: Become familiar with your law enforcement leadership and their willingness to discuss complicated situations that may occur. Take the initiative to find any search programs that may be available in your community. Be an advocate for those who have no voice and need your protection. If there is no program, look at possible ways you might facilitate movement in that direction.]

Alzheimers Organization & DC conference

The obvious support program I connected with was Alzheimer's association, Houston and Southeast Texas Chapter. I had them send me numerous pamphlets and registered to receive emails and updates that would help educate me.

Within the organization, there were kind and caring volunteers who were diligent in their efforts to answer my questions. The problem was I didn't have enough information to know what questions to ask. And in our case, other than medication therapy to slow the progression, there were no insurmountable problems in the beginning.

When I did have issues, it became apparent there was little support for persons diagnosed with Early Onset Alzheimer's or their caregivers. But, not one to give up, I was constantly trying to network with anyone who might understand our daily challenges.

As previously described, I eventually connected with a lady from Oklahoma, whose husband had Early Onset and they were our age. We emailed and spoke by phone on many occasion. In time, she provided information about her local Alzheimer's Association hosting an Early OnSet Conference. Guest speakers for this conference included members of the medical research team from Bethesda, Maryland. We registered and were given scholarship (paid registration and lodging).

At this conference, I found numerous resources and

programs. It was there I registered Dennis for the Safe Return program. Because wandering is potentially a life threatening situation, this is a government-funded program. A national information and photo database operates 24 hours a day, seven days a week, with a toll free crisis line. The program provides products such as necklace or bracelet, wallet cards, and clothing labels with the toll free 800 number. Anyone who finds a lost person calls that toll free number shown on the identification. They alert the family or caregiver listed. There is a $40 registration fee. Safe Return does not have a role in searching for a missing person or even putting out an alert. They simply kept a register of Alzheimer's persons in case they were found wandering.

We were able to meet one-on-one with the doctors after their update to the general assembly. After listening to our story, they advised us to meet with Dr. Rachelle Doody, Baylor University Research team. They believed further testing was needed, since the symptoms and conditions made them question a diagnosis of Alzheimer's.

During the final year of Dennis' life, the most meaningful connection I made as an advocate and caregiver was attending the National Alzheimer's Conference in Washington, D.C. By that time, I had a large network of fellow caregivers who wanted to know what was being done to address the research on this disease. Everyone was fed-up with this being considered a result of the aging process.

In D.C., I came prepared with my personal agenda. I created a pamphlet that I planned to share with anyone who would listen. At the conference, we met first with our state organizations. We were given clear expectations of what must be addressed at the Community, State and National levels. While in D.C. our time with congressional staff would be brief, so we would need to maximize that opportunity with a presentation of statistics and an for increased research dollars. Our Texas delegation was split into groups to meet with assigned congressional leaders.

I soon understood that my pamphlet had a mixture of appeals. My document presented our organization and the need for change. Changes I proposed included, but were not limited to Silver Alert criteria, Project Lifesaver, 911 protocol for missing persons, emergency responder training and specialized hospital care training for those caring for dementia.

The pamphlet soon became my conversation starter. Hundreds of individuals were in attendance at the various social gatherings. I did my best to speak with personnel in law enforcement, hospital administration, and various emergency responders. I networked with our state committee after their presentation of the State Plan to provide additional support for individuals with Alzheimer's.

Our small group meetings with congressional leaders did not provide me an opportunity to speak of the pamphlet, but I left one on every desk, complete with my personal contact information and website address. For that reason, the trip was a great success.

On our flight home, I sat next to a nice gentleman who asked what I was doing in D.C. I showed him my pamphlet. This started a conversation where he told me he was a neurologist who works with dementia at Michael DeBakey VA Hospital in Houston. He told me about his work and seemed quite interested in my efforts to help improve the plight of individuals/families facing the challenges. Because Dennis had VA benefits pending, he suggested I make an appointment with him even if we had to pay for the services.

All I could think was what a great week it had been to network, to be better educated and now to make this connection with a VA neurologist. Up to that point I had no interest in navigating the huge VA hospital compound. This changed my mind.

[What I learned: Networking with individuals connected with Alzheimer's/dementia is an important part of educating yourself. Don't be intimidated by the bureaucracy. YOUR LOVED ONE IS COUNTING ON YOU TO BE THEIR VOICE TO GET HELP. Caregivers are counting on someone to step into the arena of advocacy on their behalf. Any connections you make are a step in the right direction.]

Jail Bonds Court

Thanksgiving 2009 was another great time for family. We had enjoyed the usual family feast with all the trimmings. Dennis seemed to enjoy the company, but when he would wander off to the bedroom by himself, I knew it was all a bit too much. He had gotten to the place where a lot of activity made him uncomfortable. With five grandchildren in the house, it was anything but quiet.

Fortunately for me, I had everyone help decorate outside and inside for Christmas. This was a win-win for me. I had a total of 12 energized bunnies working like elves with music and ample entertainment. Dennis wanted to help, so my brother Doug found a job that the two of them could work on together. With a Chevy Chase moment, we were all finished and the lights perked up the yard with only a few glitches.

By the time kids and grandkids retreated to their respective homes, the four remaining adults were tired and ready for a relaxing evening. Doug and Beth family were still with us because this was right after Hurricane Ike and we had just finished repairs on the house.

Dennis was tired and wanted to retire for some sleep early that Sunday night. I thought it was a great idea because I knew this had been an extremely active and busy Holiday weekend for him. Doug, Beth and I settled in for a little TV time to unwind before we all went to bed.

THEN IT HAPPENED.....

About 9:00 pm, Dennis came out of the bedroom in a total rage. He rushed to the recliner where I was sitting and screamed at me in expletives and profanity declaring he was sick of all this. Initially I wasn't frightened because I had people with me. I didn't handle it the best because I said, "What are you doing? Are you trying to scare me?" Before I could say another word he dumped me backwards out of the chair, and in a split second there was total chaos.

Doug moved quickly towards Dennis saying, "Hey you can't do that to my sister!" Then the unthinkable happened. No more words. Dennis started punching my brother with incredible rage. He used Doug as a punching bag pinning him against the wall ... total rage... never pausing to our screams for him to stop. I had no choice, I called 911 because Dennis showed no sign of stopping or listening to reason.

When I got to the phone, Dennis left Doug to come toward me once again. I was hysterically asking for police to come help us calm the situation when Doug intervened once again. This time Dennis pinned him at the front door with another barrage of unceasing punches to the abdomen. The operator kept advising me to quit screaming so she could get some information. At the advice of the 911 operator, I went outside to wait for the police to arrive. I explained to the operator that Dennis had Alzheimer's and all I wanted was some help.

Once outside, I heard the sirens and saw the flashing lights in the distance. By that time, Dennis had followed me outside but was no longer punching Doug. As four

Pearland squad cars hurried to our location, Dennis went into the street screaming to just go ahead and kill him. He came by me and kept interrupting the officer who was trying to gather information. Because of his continued aggressive tone, they asked him to step back, but he refused.

Just then the officer said, "Cuff him!" What I saw then was a nightmare. About six officers chased him down in a struggle to handcuff him. He was screaming and kicking and in total rage once again. I could see in the distance, as they placed him in a squad car, that he was trying to kick out the windows of the car. One neighbor approached the vehicle and pleaded for Dennis to stop and calm down, but it continued.

After interviewing me, the officer went to my brother. He noted the aftermath of the beating and took a report for domestic violence. While they were talking, I got a true sense of how bad this situation was going to be. I got our doctor on the phone to let him know what was happening. I asked him to speak with the officer in charge. Dr. Knight confirmed the Alzheimer's diagnosis and asked that Dennis be moved to the hospital and NOT to jail for charges. The arresting officer said he had no choice but to take Dennis to jail. Hearing this just put me in a total tailspin! I couldn't think straight. I hurried to my brother to make sure he was okay. We both pleaded and explained this was a medical condition but it made no difference.

We live in a retirement community where everything is relatively quiet. You can imagine the number of caring neighbors who came outside that late night to see what was happening and to see if they could help. Now looking back, I know the officers had a terrible time managing Dennis' rage, so they certainly weren't going to take him to a hospital setting. I now understand the decision made that night.

After the police left with Dennis, we went in the house to talk with Doug. I told him how sorry I was and that if he wanted to fly back home to Iowa the next day I would make it possible. He assured me he was going no where. He said when all that happened he could see in Dennis' eyes that he was in a different place, almost like combat survival in Vietnam. Even though he was in pain, he too was concerned for Dennis. Being a brother, he just expressed over and over how glad he was that he took those punches instead of me. We both knew that I may not have survived such a powerful beating.

Then I had to make phone calls. I needed to let my kids know what had happened. I needed to call the jail to see what was going to happen. My naive way of thinking had Dennis in Pearland jail overnight and back home. I called the jail often that night and couldn't get any information other than Dennis would be moved in the morning to the Harris County Jail to be booked on two charges: resisting arrest and domestic violence. I had no idea what all that meant but I had nightmares of Dennis, in his cartoon character sleep pants, being locked up with criminals. Both of our kids had serious concerns for their dad but wanted to talk with Uncle Doug to make sure he was okay. I couldn't find adequate words to tell Doug how sorry I was about what happened. I offered to buy him a plane ticket so he could return to his home in Iowa. He declined. He understood that I would be actively seeking Dennis' release from jail as soon as possible.

I made multiple calls to the jailer checking on Dennis throughout the night. During those calls, I could hear loud shouting and metal sounds in the background. The jailer said Dennis was still exhibiting rage beating on the bars.

About 3:00 am, I got a call from a bonds company in downtown Houston. They were letting me know the charges and the cost for two bonds. I understood nothing about what they said. I just knew I would spend any amount of money to get Dennis out of jail. By 5:00 am, I was driving the streets of downtown Houston looking for this bond office. What normally would have been a frightening drive was secondary to my mission. I was alone, and in the dark of dawn, I finally found the little place set up in what looked like an old time gas station. I completed all necessary paperwork and paid the bonds thinking I could go get Dennis! WRONG. The bondsman explained I would have to wait until he was transported and booked that morning. Then I would go to the jail with these papers.

Once I was back home, I checked with the Pearland jailer to see if he had been transported. He gave me a timeline and suggested time to go to the jail. Never having had a reason to walk into any jail, I walked into the reception area for Harris County Jail expecting to be greeted in a somewhat friendly manner. WRONG again. As I told the clerk, I had the bonds paid and the details of

Dennis' medical condition. I was there to take him home. There was no sign of compassion or understanding. She said Dennis would be released later that day. She could not give me a time, he would just be released to the street.

Hearing that, I pleaded saying, "Isn't there anyone who can help me? I have to know when he will be released because he will be lost!" She suggested I go to the jail release office in another part of the building and plead my case there. Once I got to that office, I was explaining my situation and giving necessary information to the clerk when a sheriff walked in. He asked if I was inquiring about Shippey. [Thank you Jesus! Someone had seen Dennis.] He said he was in the booking unit when Dennis came through. He knew immediately something was different. After booking, he took Dennis NOT to jail but to the jail infirmary. He apologized explaining he had walked him in handcuffs and shackles. (Broke my heart). With the information I provided and seeing the situation as he had, he said he was going to meet with the psychiatrist treating Dennis in the infirmary to see if they couldn't get him released by 2:00 that afternoon. And, indeed. that is what happened.

As Dennis walked off the elevator with this sheriff, he greeted me with the hug of a child missing his mother. After signing some papers, Dennis and I were alone in the elevator headed to freedom once again. He kept asking me to look at his hands. He said, "I don't know what happened but my hands are all swollen." I assured him we were on our way to the doctor to have that checked out. During our drive to the doctor, I asked

Dennis if anyone had bothered him in jail. He said, "No, but there are some scary guys in that place. They asked me what I was in there for and I told them, 'I don't know'." That made me smile because there he was still in his cartoon sleep pants and a t-shirt.

Once we were settled at the doctor's office, the exam found only bruising and abrasions. I explained to Dennis what had happened to cause the swelling and trip to jail. He said, "NO WAY! I would never do that to Doug. I love him like a brother!" With a bit more convincing, I told him Doug would show him the wounds if he wanted. At that he bowed his head and cried, "If I am going to hurt the people I love, then I should be dead." I left Doug and Dennis to talk for a few minutes. They made their amends, but Dennis could never comprehend what had happened that tragic night.

Once I had Dennis home, I knew that was only part of the process to clear the legal action. Immediately, I had Sondra contact a lawyer she knew who understood Alzheimer's. We had a court date and Dennis would have to appear. Meeting with the lawyer to prepare the case became a problem. The first time we would meet would be court. I knew that no one knew Dennis: neither judge, nor prosecutor, nor lawyer. I knew it would be impossible to predict what he would or could say in response to the attack. I had to put the case together so the legal system understood the implications for this man. I spent almost a week compiling documents: letters from doctors, every prescription and highlighted side effects, missing persons information, etc. I presented the lawyer with a binder organized with documents to clearly articulate the case.

Included in the binder was a letter from me explaining a proactive measure to control any future violence. Mainland Hospital Institute for Living would provide the specialized medical attention and testing needed. I further explained that all legal actions must first be cleared before they would admit Dennis. I provided the court with the contact information to Mainland: doctor's name for pending admittance and the phone contact. Admittance to this unit was limited to those 65 years and older but after pleading my case, the doctor made an exception since Dennis needed specialized care and a complete evaluation of all the drugs he was prescribed.

With that binder in hand and after a short briefing in the attorney's room outside the court, our lawyer said Dennis could wait there until she met with judge and prosecutor. After waiting anxiously for a reasonable time, the lawyer returned to say we could go home. She said the binder I put together impressed the judge and prosecutor, and that they didn't need to move forward with the case. The judge had asked her to thank me for the thorough representation of this case and its complexity. They scheduled a continuance for another trial date, but Dennis did not need to appear. The only matter pending was getting legal documents and an affidavit stating Doug refused to press charges for domestic violence.

Thousands of dollars later, all charges were dropped and the case was resolved. During this short period of time, I was introduced to a foreign world of legal jockeying. I had experienced every imaginable emotion: terror, fear, anger, sorrow, disbelief, anxiety, appreciation, love, hope and faith. Faith was the strongest because I knew this was not something I could easily fix or manage. God gave me strength to endure with no fear for my own safety but only that of others.

[What I learned from this: When it comes to legal or criminal issues, be sure you have complete documentation to provide others a clear picture of the diagnosis, the medications, the side effects and other possible situations that verify the diagnosis. If you think about it, anyone can walk into court and say my loved one has dementia. YOU must provide the court system all available information pertinent to the case. My suggestion is that you keep a binder of all applicable documents as you receive them. Even things like registration tags for Safe Return are helpful. I had many documents, but they were not organized for a quick response in case of an emergency.]

Institute for Living

After the violent episode that Thanksgiving weekend, I started networking to find specialized help with management of the drugs being prescribed. At the time, I could find only one reputable program at the Mainland Medical Center, Texas City. It was not a geriatric psych unit but a well established dementia unit, Institute for Living, with a qualified team of professionals needed to assess and manage overall treatment and monitoring.

When I contacted the Institute, I was advised they would take Dennis if a spot was available AFTER all the legal action had been resolved. So after completing the judicial requirements with the case, I moved forward with our plans to have Dennis admitted to the Institute. I had been advised that the stay could take up to 21 days. Dennis was definitely not wanting to go to the hospital but I explained that after what happened with the police, we wanted to make sure his medicines were balanced properly.

The way the program was set up, we had to admit through the emergency room. Our son Scott and my brother Doug went with Dennis and me. That process alone made the admissions difficult. Dennis never liked hospitals and an emergency room is a lot of hurry and wait and wait and wait. The longer we waited, the more agitated he became. The three of us did our best to keep him distracted and calm. But by the time we got to the unit, his patience with the whole thing was gone. He wanted no part of the admission process or staying there. With his increased aggressive tone, a Code Gray was called. About four men appeared standing close by and then it happened. Dennis began screaming and saying he wasn't staying and to get him out of that place.

He moved towards me, then the team of male attendants apprehended him in a struggle. Scott sheltered me, quickly taking me by the arm through the nearest exit while I could hear Dennis screaming in the background. Once we were clear of the unit and in a secure area an explosion of sorrow came over me. Scott kept saying it would be okay, Dad would be okay, and reassured me this was the right thing to do. Within about 10 minutes a male nurse came to let me know Dennis had calmed and he was begging to speak to me. He promised them he would not become violent again. When I walked into his room, he looked like a lost frightened child. He was begging his "mother" to take him home. I kept telling him how much I love him and that he would be okay. But I explained that his medicines were all messed up and the doctors were going to help so he could go back home. With a sad look, a hug, a kiss and the words I love you, I had to turn and walk away.

I could not visit him the first seven days of his admission,. I could only call and check on how things were going. I found out that for the first four days they had to call CODE GRAY for him several times. It was so bad he was frightening the other patients, so they moved him to a more distant room. With 30 years of psych experience, charge nurse, Mike, shared that he saw more PTSD than Alzheimer's symptoms during those days. I explained that the Alzheimer's had taken him back to memories of

Vietnam. He had become obsessed reliving those days and would talk in dreams as if he were there. We had noticed that any time he saw someone with a military hat on, he would go to that person and salute them... saying welcome back. Of course the strangers were always kind and accommodating when we nodded an apology and hurried on our way.

Soon the neurologist told me about a liaison with the Veterans Administration (an advocate) who would come to the hospital and help apply for VA benefits, possibly citing the PTSD actions, for some medical and financial assistance. Frank, the VA liaison, was a great gentleman who came to the hospital with his little laptop and printer. He got all the information he needed and filled out the affidavit that was later filed on Dennis' behalf. Even though he did not think anything would be approved, he wanted to make a good faith effort to apply.

For the next 14 of 21 days, I traveled to Texas City for visiting hours. At times I would find Dennis so sedated he could barely communicate. Other times he would be sitting on the side of his bed with everything packed waiting for me to pick him up. With each visit, I tried to personalize his sparse room with family pictures, magazines and personal items from the grandkids. With staff reports weekly to update his progress, I found allies in finding the right cocktail of drugs to help this gentle and spiritual man continue living his life with the highest quality possible. I would come in at times to find Dennis at the nurse's station eating snacks for the holidays. I asked if he should be there and they all said, "Sure we have adopted him." He was settled with them and felt safe.

What I didn't realize until after it was all behind us, was that the program would heavily drug Dennis in the beginning then slowly, very slowly make adjustments that best fit his condition while maintaining quality life. With scans, it was determined Dennis had a good amount of damage to the frontal lobe where aggression is controlled. We got answers and a professional team who coached us and supported us for continued management in the home.

We celebrated our family Christmas that year without Dennis. He would return home shortly after that celebration with adjustments to previously prescribed medicines. There was an additional anxiety medication to help keep agitation and aggression at a bare minimum. I was given instructions to be proactive with this medicine. I could plan for those times when there would be more stimulation and activity in our daily lives by giving a preventative dose of medicine.

Making the decision to take Dennis to this highly specialized medical unit was purely mine with support from our kids. In fact, when we were in the ER at Mainland Medical, our personal physician called to check on Dennis. I explained we were admitting for complete evaluation. He was more than a little upset with me. We had difficult words and he certainly let me know he did not approve of that decision. That was upsetting to me because I believed it would give us a different set of eyes and a more current evaluation of the physical and mental progression of the disease. When the conversation ended, Scott assured me under no uncertain terms that this was indeed our decision and not to be concerned with that call.

Faith, hope, and love were all that carried me through those 21 days of treatment. I had faith the Institute would be current and specialized to control any future aggression. I had hope that I would be able to continue keeping Dennis at home with me. Just letting go of his day-to-day care was a huge step for me. In the end, I had to rely on God's love and sheltering comfort. It was heartbreaking to see what was happening to the man I loved.

[What I learned: As this disease progresses, you may have to make unimaginable decisions. Your emotions will most likely take you further in this care than is reasonable. But when violent behavior appears, do your best to find a hospital/doctor that specializes in patient care that monitors the changes in medication until there is some evidence of stability and control. Your safety and theirs is dependent on that decision.]

Veteran's Benefits and PTSD

Dennis applied for disability benefits from the VA based on the PTSD symptoms. The official documents were filed by Frank, the VA Liaison. We went on about our business, thinking there was no chance of any benefits, but at least we had put forth the facts.

About five months later, Dennis received a letter from the VA administration stating that his case was being reviewed. A short time later, he was scheduled for a psychiatric evaluation at Michael DeBakey Medical Facility in Houston. During that evaluation, Dennis had limited ability to give specifics about his experiences in Vietnam. The interview did not last long. As we left that appointment, I was more than sure his application would be declined. There was not enough information. The psychiatrist did, however, do a great job of evaluating what was happening with his current mental state and its connection to military.

Six months later we received a letter. Dennis was awarded 50% disability and full medical benefits. In addition, he would start receiving a monthly allotment for disability. It was a total shock - surprise - unexpected! It was timely as the medical needs were increasing for testing and monitoring the condition.

A series of initial appointments kept us traveling from one clinic to another in the huge medical complex. It was like working through a maze. Dennis was in unfamiliar settings with complete strangers as doctors. Looking back, it was stressful and disorienting for him. The pharmaceutical benefits were a huge help. Maintenance medications were prescribed and mailed to us at no cost. Extensive testing had not been updated for over six years, so the new baseline was a help to doctors.

I remember going into a neurologist appointment. This cute little doctor came into the room. She was soft spoken and gentle in her introduction to Dennis. She took all the necessary information and then excused herself. "I will be back in just a few minutes. I need to confer with our supervising neurologist regarding this case." So we waited patiently. Finally the door opened. The young doctor declared that she had someone with her that she thought I would know.

There he was..... Dr. Joseph Kass! (He was the neurologist I met on the plane traveling back from the Alzheimer's Action Summit in Washington, DC. At that time, Dr. Kass was returning from a neurologist hearing in the Senate. We struck a conversation discussing the terrible traffic getting to the airport. One thing led to another and we started discussing Alzheimer's and Dennis. He went into detail sharing his experiences and findings in the research. I came to find out that he was working with Dr. Rachelle Doody at Baylor College of Medicine in her research program AND the neurology department at VA DeBakey. He had some suggestions for future treatment. I asked how I could get an appointment with him for Dennis, but unfortunately he was taking no patients at the time.)

Dr. Kass shook Dennis' hand. He said he was personally going to take over Dennis' case because of the story we had shared on the plane. He changed a few meds, adding some and taking away others. He gave me his personal cell phone number and assured me he would be available if needed.

There are no words to describe this encounter. As always, God's plan was perfect!! Meeting Dr. K on that plane was no accident. Him coming into that exam room was divine intervention. Dennis now had one of the very best doctors available to monitor his progression into the more complicated and dangerous parts of the disease.

However, with each subsequent visit to DeBakey VA Medical Center, it became increasingly apparent that Dennis was struggling with the complexity of moving from doctor to doctor and testing sites to blood work clinics. When I could no longer manage Dennis in the various appointments, I simply continued to speak with Dr. Kass by phone and adjust medicines accordingly.

The VA benefit letters were criss crossing in their arrival and confusing at times. Dennis received a monthly check for a short time with the PTSD disability. Then a letter came stating the awarded disability was in error! The word ERROR jumped at me with alarm. Goodness gracious, what did this mean? I don't remember the exact wording but basically they were cancelling the benefits effective in 60 days. At that point it was all a blur, and my greatest fear was paying back any benefits he had already received.

I contacted the VA liaison to report the new status. He assured me he would appeal at my request. I said I wasn't concerned about an appeal but wanted reassurance that I would not have to pay back the previously awarded benefits. I did return the checks for the next two months but no further request was made by the VA. The case was closed about six weeks before Denny's passing.

[*What I learned: If your loved one is a veteran be sure to follow through on any possible benefits after active service. It is a long and tedious application process, so be prepared for long delays, but the costs for dementia care and other long term ailments can become a financial burden beyond your means. Find your nearest VA liaison to help you through that process.*]

Transition to Dementia Care Facility

There were more occasions when Dennis was readmitted to the Institute for Living to make necessary adjustments to medications that helped control aggressive behavior. Up to this point it took a village of family: daughter Sondra, grandson Ian and brother Doug, to keep Dennis at home engaged with those who loved him dearly. But even the family outings and gatherings became increasingly difficult to manage.

During a visit in October, Scott pleaded with me to place his father in a care facility, "It is bad enough we are losing Dad and we can't do a thing to stop it. But my concern now is that I don't want to lose you as well. I see the toll this is taking on you!" After Dennis assaulted Doug, both of our children expressed their concern that I do this for the family. There were sincere and emotional conversations that finally convinced me. Quite honestly, I hadn't given much thought to anything but taking care of Dennis.

In his last stay at the Institute for Living, his psychiatrist suggested it would work best to tell Dennis he was leaving the hospital for a care facility until he was better. She felt he would be more accepting of those words and that suggestion. Pine Tree Cottage was identified to be appropriate and convenient to family. Before transferring Dennis, we moved personal items to his new home. I spared no expense at making his part of the room homey and familiar. I had preferred a private room, but the director insisted he have a roommate for the initial enrollment period.

In the middle of all this, I came to the sad realization that Dennis was never coming back to our home again. There are no words to describe how that felt. During the night time hours, I waffled on the plan .... 'yes, no, maybe, not now, no never'! I had numerous conversations with our children and my siblings. I thought if I could get just one person to agree with me, I would not move Dennis out of our home for good.

My sister became a strong voice for our extended family. She explained that I would not like what she had to say, but there was no way she would agree with me regarding prolonging the placement. She said, "I am going to be your voice of reason. It is past time, way past time! You have taken such good care of Dennis long after anyone thought you should and we have all been quiet. But with the continued damage to his brain, the danger for your well-being and that of others.. it is time." She asked that I not be angry. She had been my last hope for an ally to keep him home.

So with a heavy heart, Scott, Sondra and I took Dennis to Pine Tree Cottage. He was greeted in a friendly environment that engaged him with staff and residents. He was confused but went along with my explanation that he would be staying there until he got better. Of course his obvious question, was "How long?" I didn't have the heart to say, "Forever."

We slipped out quietly, while the staff had Dennis distracted with dancing. He loved to dance so I knew he was in a peaceful state of mind. I, on the other hand, was crying with remorse and clinging to my children for support. This was one of the toughest days of my life.

[What I learned: You will need help making a decision about placing your loved one in a care facility. Make this a family decision that everyone can support. You are not doing this to them but for them and yourself. Be aware that most long term care policies will require you to pay the first 90 days before picking up payments are activated. Check your policy careful for detailed benefits of what is and what is not covered.]

Pine Tree Cottage

On numerous occasions and with every doctor visit, whether it was the medical doctor or a neurologist, I was advised to place Dennis in a care facility for about three years before I ever gave it serious consideration. I was fortunate that for those three years, my brother Doug was able to live with us and help supervise Dennis' care. But as time progressed, the agitation, aggression, and constant wandering was making it difficult for any one person to manage. During the final 12 months as caregiver/spouse, I had to give serious consideration to appropriate care facilities.

The only reason Dennis would be moved to a care facility was for safety concerns. By this time, aggressive behavior was controlled with various medications. Many facilities were limited to caring for the docile inactive senior whose needs were simply meds, food, hygiene and a place to sleep. With each visit to surrounding facilities, I had to lower my expectations for the upscale environment and focus on the personal care. With further inquiries, I found that most facilities would boot him out if there was any aggressive behavior.

Through a friend, I found a facility that was an older cottage with semi private rooms only. Nothing was fancy but the director assured me that Dennis would be well taken care of and that they could address whatever happened. Regardless of what went wrong (and many things did), I had his personal cell phone number, and we were always able to resolve issues and/or concerns.

My children and I were advised that when we left our initial visit, we should not return for at least seven days because he needed to relate to the new caregivers. He needed to trust in their care which until this time was totally with me. So when it was time to leave, he wanted to go with us. The staff did a great job of distracting him with music and dancing while we were hurried out of the building. All I remember was how I was crying and was filled with remorse and sorrow, almost a feeling of betrayal of Dennis' trust and love.

It wasn't even seven days before the staff was calling me to come for a visit. Dennis was struggling with the placement and was increasingly agitated and trying to escape. We spoke on the phone, and I assured him I would come visit soon. When I did finally see him, I wanted nothing more than to pack him up and take him home. None of this made sense to me. He should be with me 'til death do us part'. The staff and my family were encouraging, and gave me constant reassurance that this was the right thing to do.

For Dennis, privacy was not expendable. The fact that strange women were walking him into a shower room and assisting him with bathing was not something he adjusted to quickly. On more than one occasion, I was there to witness him chasing the care attendant out of the shower. But with time, his trust of their care made that hygiene concern a non-issue. Before long, incontinence made diapers a necessity. With the established trust, he didn't fight the introduction to adult diapers (because they were always referred to as briefs).

There were some heated conversations between the director and myself regarding patient care. In one very heated discussion, I remember equating our partnership much like that of a marriage. I explained that we could 'divorce' and go our separate ways but I wanted Dennis to stay there and work things out. I wanted to be an for any future residents who may be in their care. Dennis' room was moved when it was agreed there was friction between himself and roommate. (They were found throwing shoes at one another..no one knew why.) Personal care staffers were assigned and reassigned based on their ability to communicate with Dennis and keep his aggression to a minimum. One of Dennis' former swimmers donated a stationary bicycle for all residents to use.

The director later shared with me what a tremendous learning experience it was for their facility, since Dennis was one of their youngest and most physically active residents. Never before had a family taken a resident out of the facility on a regular basis. He explained that, when most residents were placed, it was because the family could do nothing with them. To the contrary, they had great difficulty managing Dennis, but when I helped, he was more cooperative and manageable. Dennis spent the last nine months of his life at the Cottage.

Rarely a night went by when I didn't lie awake wanting to go get Dennis and bring him home. The internal battle and conflicting conversations within my head were more than I could bear. All I can say is that faith in God and love of family helped me stay on this path. Nothing about this was simple.

The months came and went: Thanksgiving, Christmas, New Year's Eve, his birthday, our anniversary, Valentine's Day, St Patrick's Day, Easter and the rest. Most residents of the Cottage were prisoners to their disease and this facility. I made it perfectly clear (under great objection) that I would be taking Dennis out of the Cottage almost daily for various activities. I took him to get haircuts, beard trims, manicures, pedicures, movies, dinners, and visits with family/friends. He never wanted to go back but would do so when I explained that my brother Doug had to go home and I was working. He understood that I needed him to stay there so they could care for him so I could work. He hated it, but I believe he did it for me. He always wanted to do the right thing for me. Unfortunately, with Sondra it wasn't quite as simple. When she would return him to the Cottage, he would beg her not to take him back. That was emotionally hard on her, but she continued to include him in as many outside activities as possible.

Just a few weeks before Christmas, the Cottage accepted a new resident. She was a spry little thing who spoke like a sailor. Much to my surprise, it didn't take her long to latch on to 'her man'. During a routine visit, I walked up behind Dennis sitting at a table and leaned over to touch his shoulder and give him a hug. He was excited to see me and got up to give me a hug. All of a sudden I heard this loud and aggressive voice say, "Get your hands off my man." It took me by surprise so I just ignored the words thinking she wasn't speaking to me. As I reached for Dennis' hand to walk to a sitting room, she started to charge forward cursing and threatening that he was her husband, and I better get my hands off him. WOW!

I encouraged Dennis to join me at the Gazebo in the back courtyard. As we moved quickly out the locked door, I could hear her banging on the door and continuing her tirade. After taking some deep breaths, I said to Dennis, "That little lady thinks you are her husband." He smiled and shrugged his shoulders saying, " I know. She asked me to be her husband. I didn't ask her. I told her I don't have any money." This of course brought a smile to my face as his innocence showed in that comment. Her attention toward Dennis became so constant that the staff had to distract the lady when I came to visit. It always saddened me a bit when I would arrive to find him sitting with her (or her with him) and they would be visiting and smiling. It took time for me to get past my own sorrow, and not having my husband home to realize that if this friendship made their days a little brighter, I would just accept that as God's will. When the little lady died a few weeks later, I can honestly say I was a bit sad.

It didn't take long for the staff, our family and me to realize Dennis needed the continuous care and management of his disease. His aggression reared its ugly head on many occasions with staffers, residents and even an occasional guest. These incidents placed him in the hospital for frequent visits. Meds were adjusted, readjusted and adjusted again. He grew to love some of his caregivers because the one thing he could always sense, was people who genuinely cared for him. It was a particular incident when he head butted his Cottage manager, almost knocking her out that caused management and me great concern. This person was his strongest advocate and could always manage his mood swings up to that time.

His aggression was more like a seizure-state of mind... explosive, short, and then finished. Whether it was tossing furniture, throwing shoes at his roommate, throwing water in the face of another resident, or refusal to take medicines; it all seemed to pass quickly.

Hospice Care

Four months into Dennis' residency, management came to me requesting we put Dennis under hospice care. I was not in agreement out of my own ignorance. I didn't want to let go of the decision making process. There was no sign of immediate concerns for death, so I didn't understand why we would do this.

I didn't know what a tremendous team approach this would provide, as monitoring the dementia was becoming increasingly difficult. I was assured that I would be a key player on the team. With hospice, we had a nurse, social worker, doctor and extra care attendants as needed. In these final months, infections would cause an array of problems. Blood clots in his calves were never dissolved and that was increasingly a concern with the discoloration and swelling in his legs and feet. A hospice nurse was overseeing Dennis' daily medical needs, and a psychologist was readily available for me to address my concerns, my fears, and even my complaints. This added personnel lifted some of the burden for Dennis' care from the Cottage staff.

After hospice was assigned to Dennis' care, one of my greatest disappointments was that Dennis could no longer be sent to the Institute for Living but instead had to be taken to a Geriatric Psych Unit at a nearby hospital when his behavior could not be managed. This was the most poorly designed facility imaginable for a person with late stage dementia. First of all, with each visit he had to be admitted through the emergency room. ER staffers were well-informed regarding his late stage dementia and combative behavior. And just as expected, he caused all kinds of "hell" in the ER. It took extra personnel to contain him in a patient 'cubbie' with an arsenal of high powered injections, as we waited endless hours for a bed in the unit. On his last visit, it was so bad they lowered the head of his guerney and raised the feet because even after the nurses had administered the shots (that would take down an elephant), he continued to kick and hit and try to get out of the bed.

Once he was admitted to the unit, visitors/family could only come twice a week for a two hour period during the week and on Sundays. Dennis was with seniors who had varying psychiatric needs, therefore, he was forced into an institutional program that required all patients to attend group counseling sessions and other activities that were not suited for his condition. During his stay, Dennis became even more combative as the staff changed daily and individuals were poorly trained to address his specific challenges of dementia. Staffing for the unit was sparse at best. Dennis often had no assistance with personal hygiene so he was left in pajamas and wet or soiled briefs. On the days I visited, I personally fed him in a group dining area because if he didn't feed himself, he didn't eat. Left in this unfamiliar environment with unfamiliar faces left Dennis frightened and/or suspicious of hospital staff. In my absence, I would call to check on him. Their response would be a checklist of how he ate, how he did in group therapy, how he behaved or misbehaved with others and was he cooperative.

The frequency which Dennis was returned to the Geriatric Unit increased during the last few weeks of his life. My patience were absolutely dissolved by the insanity and insensitivity to the lack of care they provided. On one occasion, I was called to see if I would come to help with Dennis (outside visiting hours). No one could get him to bathe. And he would not let them put on the giant 'wrap-around' paper diapers. Immediately I gathered clean clothes and the briefs he was use to wearing. I was thankful they had finally listened and would let me help.

Arriving at the locked unit, I knew to push the buzzer and was promptly allowed access to this area. I went immediately to Dennis' room. He was walking out of the shower. He was so excited to see me. "Oh there you are." Just as I was dressing him in his sleep pants a nurse came in to ask why I was there and I would have to leave. Well, as you might imagine, I lost it! I explained I did not break into the unit and that I had received a phone call to come. She demanded I leave citing the rules, and I insisted I was going nowhere. She went off in a huff.

In a few minutes, a security officer, accompanied by a professional looking lady, appeared at the door. I looked up and said, "I think I know why you are here." She introduced herself as the managing director over the hospital. I didn't give her time to speak further but interrupted to explain all that had happened and why I was there. I explained the difficulties they were having and why it was so important for me to be there and help. She acknowledged my concerns and the situation and suggested that in the future I call for a supervisor or administrator to express my concerns. As I look back now, I am sure it wasn't as smooth as that just sounded but I got my point across and stayed with Dennis for a few hours until he napped.

During subsequent visits, I found Dennis wandering around the locked unit, looking for a way out. On more than one occasion, I found him picking at door locks, hoping to find the right combination to freedom. Another time, I found him with no glasses (he was blind without them). I asked the nurse what had happened to his glasses. She said they were in his bedside table .. broken. She guessed he had sat on them. No one had notified me of this problem or I would have brought him an old pair. (It goes without saying, communication from the hospital was poor at best.) I promptly assured Dennis his glasses would be replaced. At the end of our visit, I walked him back to his room and asked if he wanted anything more. He smiled and said, "Yes, I would like to see my mom". I was taken back by that request because his mother died five years earlier. I hugged him oh so gently and said I would see what I could do.

When Dennis left that facility one last time, I vowed I would meet with the Administrator over this unit to discuss detailed ways they could address the needs of dementia care and how to work more closely with their family/caregiver. That meeting took place shortly after Dennis' release. Also in attendance were the admissions director and a social worker. They listened attentively and seemed genuinely interested in my ideas. I left that meeting with a feeling of accomplishment. I had given a voice to those who needed it most .. the patient.

[What I learned: Pick your dementia care facility carefully. Ask questions regarding: who is on duty during night hours for any emergency medication needs; what are the visitation guidelines; how do they manage aggressive behaviors; what social activities are scheduled, and can you continue providing the medications or do they require individually wrapped drugs from their selected pharmacy. (Individually wrapped meds have excessive pricing.)

Hospice care provides a team-oriented approach to expert medical care, pain management, and emotional and spiritual support tailored to the patient's needs and wishes. They provide needed drugs, medical supplies, and equipment. A hospice physician, nurse, health aides, social workers and clergy are among those who team with the family to meet the patient's individual needs. Your loved one will be assessed to see if their medical condition warrants hospice care. Even after it is provided, it can be removed if the patient improves.]

Journey's End

In one of many meetings with Cottage staffers, it was brought to my attention that Dennis was combative when they woke him during the night to change his briefs. His behavior was such that they strapped him in a chair until he calmed down. Strapping him down only escalated the behavior. Once this was brought to my attention, I asked that the director and hospice nurse meet with me to explain in more detail. They were waking him from a sound sleep and it startled him. I insisted they NOT wake him but to let him sleep. According to their state guidelines, they had wake him every two hours to make sure he was dry. My prompt response was I would sign a release or even have a lawyer draw up a document to let him sleep. It seemed simple enough to me, and I expected my demands to be honored. Only in extreme cases should Dennis be strapped to a chair.

As a result of that meeting, the charge nurse on the night shift was notified of that decision. She was not happy but she had no choice. A few days later, early in the morning, Dennis was found on the floor, face down with knees drawn under him. He had been in that position most of that night. The charge nurse said she was just following orders to leave him alone. When the morning shift checked on Dennis, his face was swollen and he was unable to help them move him. An ambulance was called, and he was rushed to the hospital. During that short stay, our doctor determined that Dennis had rhabdomyolysis. (As defined in Wikipedia, this is a condition in which damaged skeletal muscle tissue breaks down rapidly. Breakdown products of damaged muscle cells are released into the bloodstream; some of these, such as the protein myoglobin, are harmful to the kidneys and may lead to kidney failure. The severity of symptoms, which may include muscle pains, vomiting and confusion, depends on the extent of muscle damage and whether kidney failure develops. The muscle damage may be caused by physical factors (e.g. crush injury, strenuous exercise), medications, drug abuse, and infections. The numerous hospital visits due to kidney failure, blood clots and infections had caused his body to break down to a point of no return. There was a lengthy discussion regarding end of life comfort care. My first thought was to take Dennis home to die. But as a family, we decided to have him returned to the Cottage.

We were advised Dennis would live no more than 7-10 days. It was going to be comfort care for his final days. Scott, Sondra and I waited patiently as Dennis was transported back to the Cottage. I made a quick call to Dennis' best friend and he came immediately. The kids and I said our final words for the day and Dennis was listening but not speaking much. Then Bruce walked in the room.

When Bruce arrived, he walked immediately to Dennis and reached out with a handshake and his old familiar greeting .. "Hey what's up partner?" Dennis came to life with a lunge towards his friend as they shared a barrage of expletives about who could beat who in the water. The kids and I watched in amazement as these two best friends shared what would be their final words. Within a short period time (just minutes), Dennis leaned back into the bed to rest. He was quiet. Bruce turned to us

126

with a puzzled face and said, "I think I just wore him out with that arm wrestling exchange we just had. I wasn't sure if he was happy or mad at me." Of course we were accustomed to his familiar sense of humor with Dennis. It wasn't long thereafter that the hospice staffers were arriving to take over care of Dennis.

Later after everyone had left, Dennis was given his morphine and he was resting peacefully, I asked him if he still wanted to go see his mother (deceased) and he responded without hesitation, "Yes". I told him I thought it was a great idea and we were busy making arrangements for that to happen. He smiled. Thinking I would have 7-10 more days to say my goodbye, I could say no more. I remember lying awake that night crying softly and praying for mercy. I prayed for mercy for Dennis and myself. I could not begin to imagine watching this dying process for the next few days. As it worked out, we were called back to his bedside in the early hours of the morning. Before we even got there -- he had passed. He lived only eight hours in hospice. As difficult as it was to accept, God had answered my prayers. His timing was merciful for Dennis and myself and our family.

I remember walking into his room. There lay the body of this man who I loved so dearly. But it was just that -- a body. His soul, the essence of his being, had crossed over to eternity. He was gone. I wept quietly as I kissed his forehead.

We all waited quietly for the funeral home to come pick up the body. A young man walked in with a gurney. He introduced himself, then looked over to the body and said, "There is my coach." With that comment he explained that he swam for Dennis at Dobie High School. He told stories of admiration for him. The most endearing story was when he spoke of his daughter who was now a swimmer. He said when she isn't happy with her swim, he asks her if she did her best. If she did that's all that mattered. He said that's what I learned from Coach.

Brain Donation

One year before Dennis passed away, I knew we wanted to donate his brain for research. Much of what was happening did not make sense. There were too many unanswered questions. So while I was sitting by his side during the nine weeks of hospitalization (IV therapy from failing kidneys and blood clots), a good friend researched possible brain donor foundations.

What she found was there was no program in Texas and very few in the United States who were even interested in taking the donation. There were, of course, medical schools interested in the cadaver but nothing was found providing research and possible answers. This was more than a little frustrating, but for the time, I let it rest.

Then in the spring of 2011, I had the opportunity to interview for the Alzheimer's Ambassador Program in Houston. During the interview, I was met by the Public Relations officer for the Houston Chapter. I found that I would have personal contact with targeted members of Congress, building relationships with decision-makers and their staff and holding them accountable to their commitment to fighting Alzheimer's. He detailed the responsibilities and commitment involved.

The interview went well and before leaving, the Ambassador Coordinator and I discussed personal experiences and concerns I had trying to find a place for brain donation. To my amazement, he was excited to give me contact information for the Sports Legacy Institute.

Sports Legacy Institute in Boston, MA. was founded by Chris Nowinski and Dr. Robert Cantu in reaction to new medical research indicating that brain trauma in sports had become a public health crisis. Post-mortem analysis of the brain tissue of former contact sports athletes revealed that repeated brain injuries could lead to neurodegenerative disease known as Chronic Traumatic Encephalopathy. Mr. Nowinski had recently been in Houston and spoke to the Texas based delegation soliciting brain donations. In particular, they were looking for individuals who were athletes with Alzheimer's/dementia. It was just a matter of making contact with the donor office, and within less than a week, all the necessary documents were completed.

I left the Ambassador interview knowing it was not a program I wanted to serve. Being Ambassador was more of a political position to help raise funds, facilitate legislative awareness and communicate with legislators for further development of research. My interests were clearly to act as an advocate promoting improved community support for family needs, hospital care, emergency response and community support. I declined the offer.

This is what I call one of those "God moments". It was such a huge relief to know that something good could come from all this. As an educator, I knew something might be gained by taking part in the research. Certainly Dennis had no head trauma that I was aware of, but the Institute was excited to get their first "swimmer" donation. This all happened just six weeks before Dennis passed. Timing was everything. By the grace of God, our family and others would benefit from what might be found.

So it was the morning of Denny's passing, the Cottage made all the necessary contacts to the funeral home and to the Sports Legacy Institute. Dennis was transferred first to the funeral home where his body was picked up the Pathology lab assigned to this case. His brain was harvested and body returned in less than 12 hours so all normal arrangements for the family could be scheduled.

After the donation was received, Dr. Robert Stern, Neurologist with the research team, contacted me for an interview. He explained the research process and sent critical release forms for all of Denny's medical records. After he received all the medical documents, he held an 90+ minute conference interview with me. We discussed detailed background questions, experiences, behaviors and all other information gleaned necessary to provide valid feedback.

Dr. Ann McKee, Pathologist, would be leading the research team, dissecting and investigating our brain donation. She would take the donation "in the blind" not knowing anything about the person, only a number assigned to the specimen. Dr. Stern's role was to collect all the information available regarding medical treatment, behaviors and life experiences. When all necessary data was completed by these two researchers, they would meet to put together a report of their findings; how it connected both with the physical specimen and the medical background. This total process took over eight months.

I received a notice that a conference call with the research team was being scheduled. Scott, Sondra, Dennis' brother Steve, Dennis' best friend Bruce and I were all connected into the conference call. While waiting for the call that day, I was trying to stay calm but couldn't contain my anxiety. My biggest concern was for our children and grandchildren. There was NO known Alzheimer's in Dennis' family history, so where had this come from?

The phone rang. The conference started. Each of us had received a highly scientific three page autopsy report of findings. The goal was to go over the report and answer all questions. Much of what was shared in the beginning was lost to me with no scientific understanding of the terms. But then it came!!! This I did understand. Dennis did NOT have Familial Alzheimer's. He had trauma induced dementia CTE.

Much discussion followed in answer to questions. What Dr. McKee shared was that she was sorry that they didn't have more answers. She said Denny's brain pathology brought up more questions than answers. She said his donation was critical to further investigation. They were extremely appreciative of our sacrifice, but to me, we were the one's who were appreciative. Dennis had always stayed in denial of the Alzheimer's diagnosis. He definitely had dementia and what we found out was regardless the cause, his dementia would have been treated basically the same.

Our personal neurologist read the pathology findings and was not surprised. During the ten years of treatment, he was always concerned with the diagnosis, but obviously had to treat the dementia. He said they are learning so much more about CTE injuries and, for Dennis, it may have very well happened in Vietnam. [Dr. McKee had mentioned that they have findings of CTE with military service in Iraq and Afghanistan.] Regardless of where it happened or how it happened, I thank the good Lord my children do not need to be overly concerned with the genetics of Alzheimer's. It was a cloud they would have lived under forever had we not made the donation.

[What I learned: Make every effort to donate your loved one's brain for research to further the development and understanding of future treatment needs. An autopsy at a cost of about $1500 will solidify the diagnosis of Alzheimer's. Yes or No. That is important to the family. But with reputable research, you will have a more detailed report and the satisfaction that you are part of the solution with this donation.]

Legacy of the Coach

Before I share the tribute that was given by a former swimmer at Dennis' Memorial in Houston, I want to go back and share the Swimmers' Reunion we hosted when Dennis retired.

It was a birthday surprise in February 2004. We started early in the fall spreading the word. Then I was blessed to find Scott, one of Dennis' former swimmers who was a professional webmaster. He took the information and created a beautiful website honoring coach and inviting swimmers from years past to his retirement celebration.

The best part on the website was individuals having the opportunity to send Dennis a personal message of congratulations. And on the same site were instructions regarding registration for the dinner event here in Bella Vita Ballroom.

I had decided that with the progression of dementia, the best celebration for Dennis was not just to have adult friends and coaches honor his years of service, but for those he touched daily to have that opportunity. With great excitement, we saw the numbers of registrations grow beyond expectation. Former athletes and former swim parents came from miles around here in Texas. Others flew in from other around the country.

When Dennis returned home late January, I told him what we were doing. His excitement was all I needed to know this was the right decision. Each day I would give him an update of who was coming. And of course, I could not leave out the Athletic Director and High School Principal (both friends) who had supported Dennis and stood behind him when the end of his career was evident.

We hosted the tribute, and friends from Bella Vita served the catered dinner menu. There were stories told of years past and a great deal of laughter as those in attendance poked fun at their beloved coach and themselves. That retirement party was a great success thanks to webmaster Scott, our daughter-in-law Melissa who took reservations, and all those who were in attendance.

Ironically, it was many of these same swimmers (40+ years old) who visited Dennis in the hospital and who attended his final farewell - The Celebration of Life.

Now I will share with you the eulogy written and spoken by Susan Stevens Langlois (former student and swimmer). It speaks volumes to the man that Dennis was -- coach, mentor, advisor, parent and spiritual leader.

"Everyone remembers Coach, even those who did not know him personally. He was a master swimmer, achieving many victories throughout his lifetime. He could be seen riding his bike to work, swimming in his off time, working on swim schedules during lunchtime and picking up trash in and around the pool area at any given time. That's how he lived his life.

But those of us who swam under Coach's leadership, will remember him in a more profound, endearing, infinite way. Coach was a man of few words, but it's not what Coach said that he will be remembered for. It's what he didn't say.

In fact, it's what Coach Shippey DID that will be his legacy. It's how he lived his life. Coach was a leader, leading by example, instead of lectures. He lived his life each day, honoring his values of mutual respect, perseverance and commitment to excellence in everything he did. Always.

Coach was a cheerleader when we raced, a drill sergeant when we slacked off, a teacher if we needed lessons, a boss if we rebelled and a friend when we graduated. It's how he lived his life. Much of what we learned about how to live life, we learned in high school, through Coach's example.

Although he was not a talkative man, we knew when Coach was proud of us, concerned about us, upset with us and we also knew that he honestly loved coaching us. We knew. His actions always spoke so much louder than his words. It's how he lived his life.

Just recently, I began reflecting on what Coach Shippey meant to me at this point in my life, almost three decades after graduating. And what I realized is that - unknowingly, I had taken him with me after I graduated, through college and all through my twenty six years in education. Coach has been here with me all along, in the shape of a mentor, a cheerleader, a drill sergeant, a teacher, a boss and a friend – to my own students. Because the way he lived his life, in many ways became the way I tried to live MY life.

Each one of us knows which part of Coach we took with us after graduation. And we know which part will stay with us, living on, living in us.

This is Coach's legacy - that he will live on in all of us here in this room, in some way, shape or form. Now and always.

At some point today, as you reminisce with those in attendance, look closely at their character, listen closely to their attitude - you will find Coach. He's here. Now, and always.

We will miss you, Coach Shippey. The victories in your life were many, but your final victory is the sweetest of them all - where the pool water is always crystal clear, the roads are always paved, your pain has fallen away and your spirit has been restored."

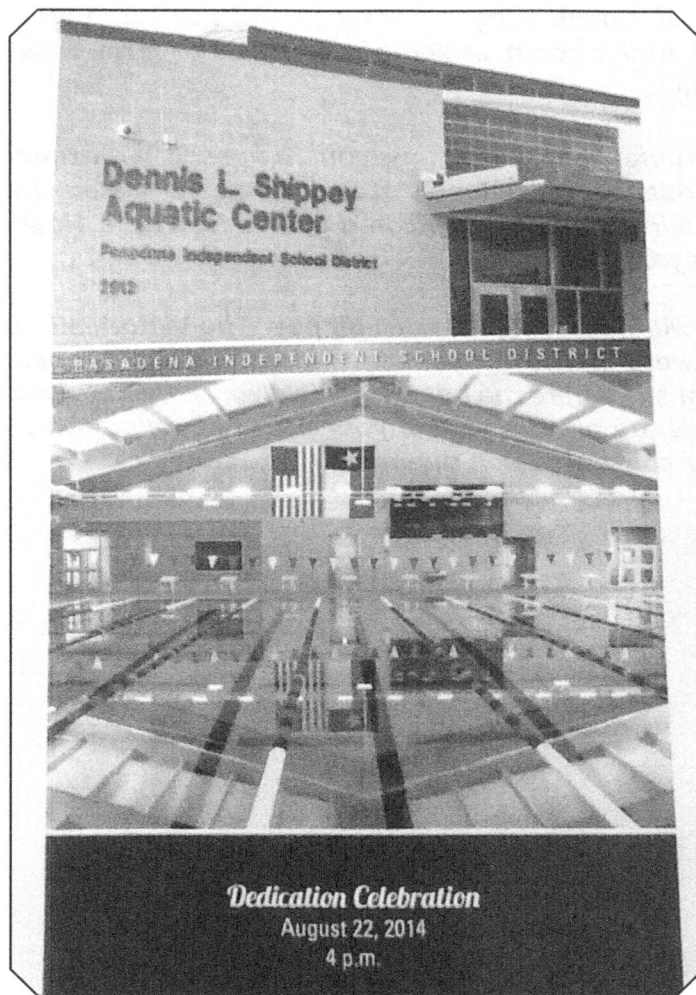

Dennis L. Shippey
Aquatic Center
Pasadena Independent School District
2013

PASADENA INDEPENDENT SCHOOL DISTRICT

Dedication Celebration
August 22, 2014
4 p.m.

Brochure from the dedication of the
Dennis L. Shippey Aquatic Center
Pasadena, Texas
August 22, 2014

About the Author

Linda Moorman Shippey holds a Masters Degree in Education from the University of Houston, at Clear Lake, Texas. She has dual residence in Pearland, Texas and Davenport, Iowa. She is now retired from Pasadena Independent School District in Pasadena, Texas.

Before Mrs. Shippey was a school administrator, she was a mathematics teacher grades six through junior college. Her expertise is not that of a writer. It was with great reluctance she was ready to tackle the daunting task of writing for others to critique. But with a compelling need, she has told her story.

Dennis L. Shippey, her husband, was diagnosed in May 2002 with Early Onset Alzheimer's and lost that battle in August 2011 from what was later determined to be a CTE (chronic traumatic encephalopathy).

From the beginning, she realized there was little information readily available to the caregivers who were facing the challenges of this diagnosis. Through a series of complex and sometimes dangerous situations, she learned the hard way how to find the appropriate support. She learned what adjustments to make for daily living. She learned how to maintain the best quality of life for her husband, for as long as possible. And at the same time, she recognized the missing components for having effective emergency responders, medication adjustments, hospital staffing and community programs along the way.

Even though this story floated in her mind from 2011 to 2016, Mrs. Shippey could not get it off her mind. Now the story has been told. This is a story to be shared with family, friends, organizations and senior groups who may be facing dementia care or will in the future.

Being a caregiver for all those years took its toll on her physical and emotional well-being. Linda would warn others to take advantage of respite opportunities and counseling whenever possible. After struggling two years to find her new normal, she slowly came to understand the blessings and the lessons learned, that came as a result of this journey.

Recently, Mrs. Shippey reconnected with a man she was briefly engaged to in 1968. As the story goes, Dennis and John Berry had been good buddies and playmates in kindergarten/first grade. They knew each other long before either knew Linda. John and Linda are now in a committed and loving partnership. Together, they enjoy handcrafting crosses made of various types of wood, jewelry and discarded items from the tool chest.

If you know of a family, friend or organization that would like to have this story told and/or discussed in more detail, please email lsshippey@yahoo.com.

Appendix:

Highlights from the Washington DC brochure

- To change the Texas Silver Alert: With this change, individuals would not need to meet the age 65 requirement for broadcast
- To promote Project LifeSaver: With this initiative, efforts will be made to find programs like Project LifeSaver to assist in tracking individuals who wander from the safety of their home. PLS is just one tracking program that could be the first respondent for a person who wanders.
- To improve 911 Protocol: With this initiative, no one should ever hear a 911 operator response "This is not an emergency. Please hang up and call your local police department." A protocol should be in place to channel that call to the appropriate response team.
- To address legal challenges: It is imperative that appropriate training and education programs target emergency law enforcement responders for Alzheimer's related situations such as wandering and/or safety to self and others.
- To improve hospital training: It is inevitable that your loved one will be in the hospital for various afflictions. During those late stages of dementia, most hospitals are ill-staffed to provide appropriate care and monitoring for the patient. Even geriatric-psych units that are designed to address the psychological challenges of aging are not meeting those needs. When establishing a specialized unit for hospital needs for dementia patients, hospital administrators would be wise to work cooperatively with families that are managing those needs on a day-to-day basis.

CPSIA information can be obtained
at www.ICGtesting.com
Printed in the USA
LVOW03s1100310517
536403LV00001B/14/P